Business

Plan

Analysis

"Chemical Industries"

Harmaizar Zaharuddin

Business Plan Analysis
"Chemical Industries"

By: Harmaizar Zaharuddin
Editor of Indonesia language
Novie Firly Silviana, SP
Translated by : Jenika Group Ltd

Publisher Company: **CV Dian Anugerah Prakasa**

Complex Permata Hijau Permai Blok D4 No. 8, North Bekasi, Bekasi 17125, West Java, Indonesia.

Telephone : (+6221) 68457161, 92771943
Mobile   : (+62) 0812-9605245

Cooperating with
Jakarta Investment Consulting (JIC)
Email: harmaizar@yahoo.com, dian_dap@yahoo.com

1st Edition, January 2009

Business Plan Analysis "Chemical Industries"

By: Harmaizar Zaharuddin

Copyright@ 2008, to Harmaizar Zaharuddin, Complex Permata Hijau Permai Blok D4 No. 8, North Bekasi, Bekasi 17125, West Java, Indonesia.

National Library:
ISBN / CIP (Catalog In Publication)

Business Plan Analysis " Chemical Industries"
The publisher Team: Dian Anugerah Prakasa, Ed. I., Bekasi
viii + 92 pages; 5.25 x 8 in

ISBN   : 9799799449
EAN-13 : 9789799799449
   I.   Business Plan Analysis "Chemical Industries"
   II. The publisher Team Dian Anugerah Prakasa

INTRODUCTION

Global crisis is causing many people getting termination of employment. This condition makes me feel to find out its solution in order that they can get out of difficulties. One of them is appealing society to establish own business. Besides that, many people do not know, based on writer's experiences and observation, ways of starting a business professionally. Most people started a business autodidactically that finally came up against fiasco.

In American, it is proven by history that establishing a business professionally is successful of keeping it in the first year 96% and 94% lasting up to the fifth year. Experienced people establishing a new business is capable of maintaining it 15%-20% in first year. It shows that establishing a business professionally is very important and the contribution of Business Plan Analysis is very large in building a business. (Source: Book of Financial Revolution, Author Tung Desem Waringin).

Moreover, writer's experiences in applying the concept of Business Plan Analysis in the length of service as Business Plan Manager succeeded expanding a business from asset ± US$ 12,500,000 (1 Company) becoming ± US$1,000,000,000 (15 Companies) within ± 5 years. Up to 15 years ahead those companies still exist and none of them is closed yet, that is Eterindo Wahanatama Ltd. Plc. (ETWA).

By publishing this book I hope gratefully that I can help the society in building and expanding their business.

January 2009

Author

LIST OF CONTENTS

CHAPTER II Economic and Marketing Aspect

CHAPTER III   Project Aspects

CHAPTER IV   Investment and Management Aspect

CHAPTER V Financial Aspects

FORM AND APPENDICES

CHAPTER V Financials Aspects

_____

PART ONE
TECHNIQUE

BUSINESS PLAN
ANALYSIS

TECHNICQUE

I. Ways of Applying Business Plan Analysis

So that you get easy applying Business Plan Analysis, there are 3 ways, namely:

1. Understanding IACM Map (See picture 1 IACM) which is the first steps to apply Business Plan Analysis. And then you have to understand Format Proposal map (See Picture 2), it is the result composition format of Business Plan Analysis in order that other people will get easy to understand it.

2. Reading entirely this book. This can give an illustration and facilitate you to apply Business Plan Analysis for your business.

3. In each Chapter on Format Proposal, the matters need to be paid attention to, are:

   A. **Chapter I Business Legality**. In this part what you have to do is collecting the data of business policy, such as: license fee, policies and tax rate. Meanwhile the arrangement of the license will be conducted after whole other parts are completed being analyzed and stated being beneficial.

   If you will build a quite large business, analysis examples in this book, then, can represent it or be made compatible with the conditions needed in your country. But if it's a small business, some parts may be wiped off.

   B. **Chapter II Marketing**. This part is very important and must extra-prudent in carrying out it. Unclear analysis' aims or wrong direction in carrying out the analysis will have fatal result and put your business operational at risk. As we know marketing is the spearhead of company.

Flow Chart - Process of Business Plan Analysis

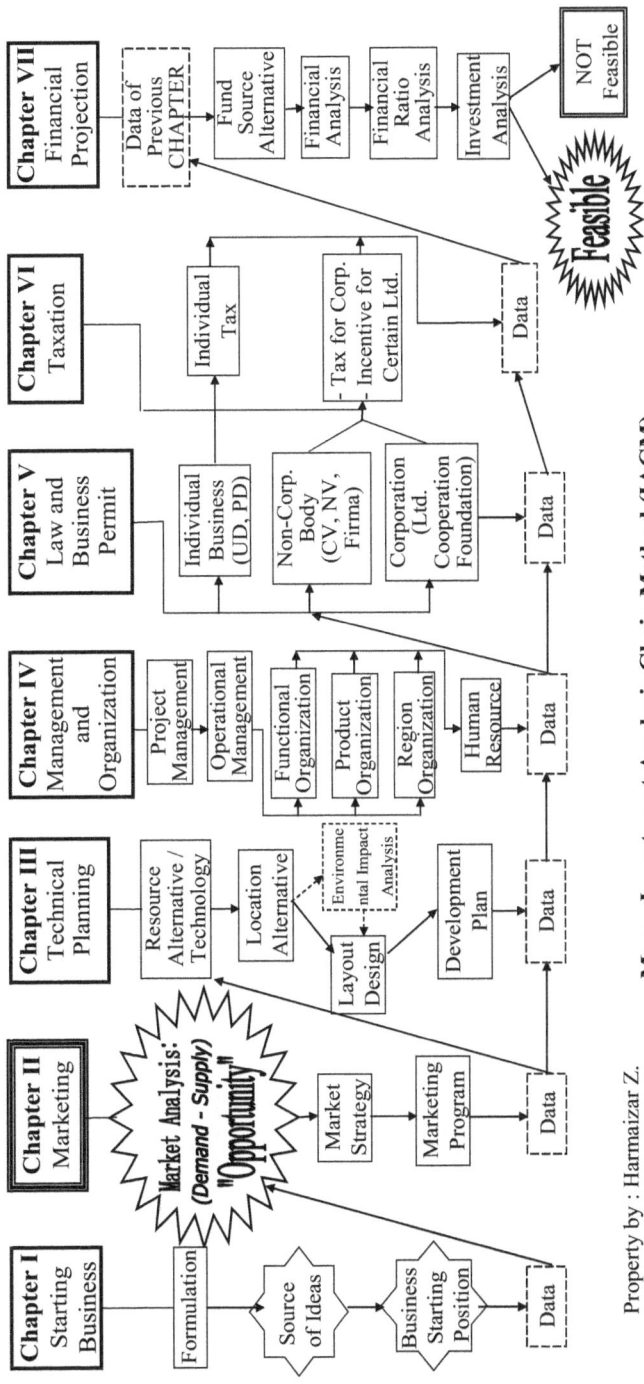

Property by : Harmaizar Z.

Map – Investment Analysis Chain Method (IACM)

Explanation of each step in map, Please Read Book "A to Z Entrepreneur in Practice"

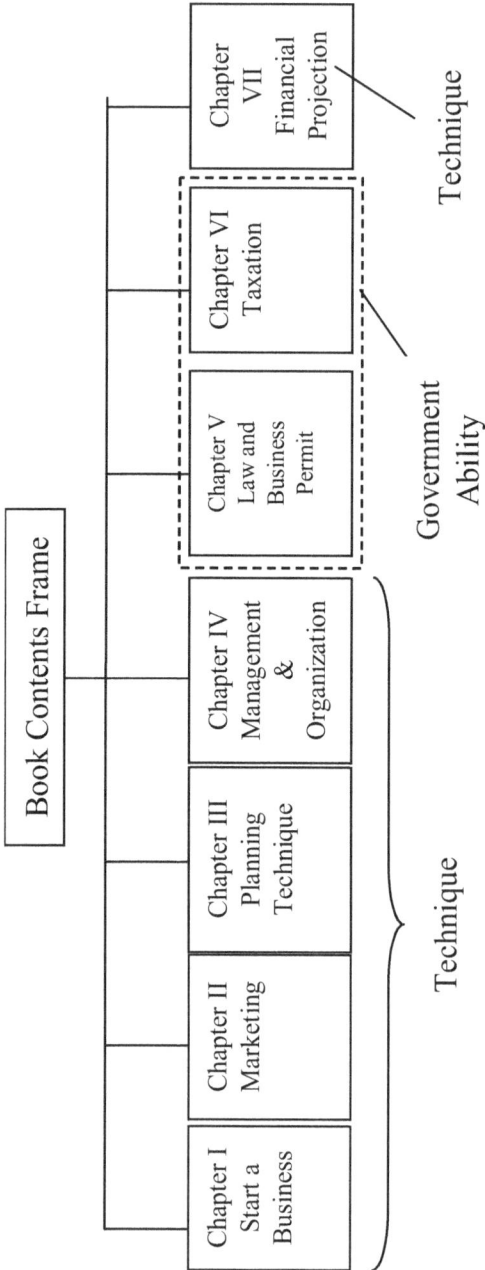

Picture - 2 Format Proposal Business Plan

Steps in marketing analysis are:

b. **Product**. You must know well what kind of products you will trade, such as its benefits, product's life span or its source.

c. **Market Segmentation**. At this part you must distinctly aim market; there are 2 very important factors that must be considered. Which market shall you target? There 2 options, namely: **Industry market** or **Consumer market**. With **Geographical scale**: International, National, Provincial, sub district, village or citizens association (RW) scale. Especially for Consumer market **Demographical scale** will also need being analyzed, namely: Age, Religion, Economic standard or all levels. After you choose the aimed market segmentation, for instance: consumer market, marketing area of a province, product for 15 – 20 year-old, so then the next step is:

d. **Demand and Supply.** At this part you must look up the historical demand's data that is quantitative for minimal 5 years and projected for 5 – 10 years, namely, the data of total children under 15 – 20 year-old in a province. You must also seek the historical supplier's data that provides the products and the progress of supplier / competitor.

e. **Opportunity.** After you obtain the historical data and Demand and Supplier Data are projected so you will get easy to analyze the large of projection of your product market's opportunity.

Notes:

Historical Data is necessary for large companies minimal 5 years (1 period = 1 year), for small companies 1 – 3 years (1 period = 1 month, 1 semester)

Data Sources can be obtained from Central Bureau of Statistics (BPS), Department of Industry, sub-district, Head of Village, village or citizens association (RW) and neighborhood association (RT).

Marketing Strategy

After you find out about the large of entire market opportunity and considering the existence of competitors, and then you can, in the next step, analyze market strategy so as to get the largest market portion.

C. **Chapter III Technical**. At this part shall be taken into account are: Location selecting, used Technology, Product Sources / Raw Material, Lay-out Design of business place, availability of infrastructure and utilities (electricity, water, etc).

D. **Chapter IV Management & Organization.** Besides you have to design a good Management & Organization Structure, you also have to heed available human resource; this is related with location selecting.

E. **Chapter V. Financial Projection.** At this part you must analyze comprehensively, by collecting quantitative data from chapter I up to chapter IV and financial data, such as: the policies of debts and credit, stock, interest rate, debt portion, etc. Further analyzing financial projection 1 - 10 years it depends on the large of business.

II.   Financial Projection & Microsoft Excel Program

In building a business it's very crucial to understand how to analyze financial projection because financial projection is an analysis instrument that will determine whether that business is qualified or unqualified to be established. Without understanding financial projection we will search around for running company operation, especially with the tightest situation of competition where you have to analyze promotion costs, minimal sell target having to be obtained, price discount in detail etc.

Writer is realized that to analyze financial projection is quite complicated and not all people can do that, in fact many people having a financial background are also not capable of analyzing financial projection and on top of that those who do not have a financial background.

Therefore, to make easy analyzing financial projection, we need an auxiliary apparatus, namely, computer program. Actually programs for financial projection having set up and ready to use are much available in market, as being set up in Visio Basic language, but the most are partial and not comprehensive, and many programs are not suitable as well with the needs of business that we shall build.

In order that readers are able to make computer program – financial projection and get easy to modify it according to necessities, hence we shall talk over Microsoft Excel, which is a simplest-operated computer program.

For making easier, writer will give FREE financial projection program by using the language of Microsoft Excel for **Chemical Industries** business. And all you have to do here is change names, investment values, and financial variable.

A. FREE Financial Projection Program

For getting this program there are some steps, namely:

1. Scanning the proof of book selling or the receipt, send to Email: **dian_dap@yahoo.com.**

2. We shall reply immediately after we check it, 2 weeks at the latest.

3. Password of the program is **280775nv1250865hz**

4. For operating it or understanding it profoundly, please read the next sub-chapter. Or

5. Download at **www.harmaizar.com** but the program is setting up.

B. Production Services for Financial Projection Program

When you don't have time to study and make a financial projection program, we would like to offer you to set up the program according to your business necessities (all kinds of business) but it is charged to the amount of US$ 600. And all data come originally from you. The steps are:

1. Transferring the fee 100%

   No. Acc.: 79441416

   Holder: Harmaizar

   Danamon Bank, Branch Menara Bank Danamon, Jakarta, Indonesia (Swift Code = BDINIDJA).

2. Giving me the information of the fee and kind of business will be build by SMS, Mobile Phone 0812-9605245 or Email: dian_dap@yahoo.com.

3. I will send you a blank form to be filled out with needed costs data and financial variable, and then resend it to us.

4. We shall immediately work on it $\pm$ 1 week.

Benefits:

· You can use benefits of this program for your other business and of the same kind, either for business expansion or new business building in other location.

· You can also change the data by yourself, may be you get new information, such as: investment products' price, interest rate, etc.

III.   Advantages of Business Plan Report

Advantages of the result report of business plan analysis are:

1. Initiator. Knowing whether a business going to be build is beneficial or not.

2. Other Prospective Shareholders. To look for business partners and support lack of funds or to share good fortune / risks.

3. Banks or Non-Bank Institutions. To seek funds for the lack of funds in developing the business.

4. Governmental Agencies. That related with permits and facilities (incentive) shall be provided.

VI. Financial Projection Design

In this sub chapter will be discussed about financial projection preparation method at company (new investment) establishment plan, especially at trading and distribution business sector. Steps taken in financial projection preparation:

A. Data Collection

Data required based on survey result and analysis which have been explained in the previous chapters, namely:

1. Determination on investment amount.

2. Determination on portion and loan interest amount
   - Investment loan portion
   - Working Capital loan portion
   - Long term loan interest (interest on investment loan)
   - Short term loan interest (interest on working capital loan)

3. Factors determination which influencing working capital amount:
   - Average loan period
   - Average debt period
   - Average goods supply
   - Average cash requirement is operational cost which needed from the beginning of material purchasing up to claim for payment on goods selling.
   - Cash and bank minimum for keeping unwanted fluctuation costs.

4. Determination on fund source

5. Determination on Sales Volume

6. Determination on product selling price

7. Determination on product principal price

8. Determination Operational Cost amount

9. Determination on depreciation and amortization method based on prevailing law, whether representing regular company or Foreign / Dometic investment company which have obtained BKPM's facility.

10. Determination on income tax based on current law, this related with business form (private or entity) Ltd. (Regular, Foreign / Domestic Investment, and Public) and also related to facility from government or BKPM (The Investment Coordinating Board).

B. Preparation Process

Then after the data above collected already, then we could start preparing financial projection, financial projection preparation should be made by using computer program, such as: **Lotus** or **Microsoft Excel**. Sample of financial projection could be seen at **Proposal preparation sample** in attachment of this book (page 59 -88).

If financial projection preparation with computer program, then will be easier to carry out simulation **try** and **error** within 5-15 minutes, by changing investment cost, selling price, product price and various financial assumptions (further about sensitivity analysis could be seen in the next sub chapter).

Financial projection preparation process divided into 3 steps, namely:

First Steps is preparing specification of financial projection calculation, namely:

1. Construction Cost Schedule Preparation

   This has been discussed in Chapter III about permanent investment and in Chapter V about financing schedule and Interest During Construction. (See Case Study).

2. Investment and Reinvestment Projection

   See sample of financial projection attachment proposal at Appendix-07

3. Depreciation and Amortization Projection

Variable which be considered is depreciation and amortization method which used or permitted. For clearer explanation could be seen in sample of financial projection Appendix-08.

4. Selling Projection

Variable which be considered:

- Selling price projection

- Sales/production volume projection

- Loan average ratio

- Inventory average ratio

See sample of financial projection attachment proposal, Appendix-05

5. Cost of Goods Sold Projection

Variables which be calculated:

- Sales volume projection

- Cost of Goods Sold projection

- Import duty policy, if goods imported projection

- Inventory average ratio

See sample financial projection attachment proposal, Appenidx-04

6. Operational Cost Projection

Calculated from data obtained in first year, then pulled ahead by considering Sales (production) volume increase, cost of goods sold and inflation.

See sample of financial projection attachment proposal at Appendix-09.

7. Loan and Interest Payment Projection

Variables which need to be calculated:

- Number of investment fund

- Loan portion

- Loan interest

See sample of financial projection attachment proposal, Appendix-06

8. Working Capital Requirement Projection

   In this context calculated working capital requirement at operation period initial and further period. If at further period, significant sales development estimated will be the cause of working capital shortage. Then it's necessary to calculate additional working capital at the next/further period.

   Calculation method of working capital requirement at initial and period operation, furtherly could be seen at financial attachment at Appendix-10

Second Step:

After having completed projections preparation. then further step preparation of **Main Financial Projection Report**, based on previous projections above, namely:

9. Profit and Loss Projection

   See sample of financial attachment proposal Appendix-03

10. Cash Flow Projection

    See sample of financial projection attachment proposal, Appendix-02

11. Balance Sheet Projection
    See sample of financial projection attachment proposal Appendix-01

Third Step is carrying out some analysis and financial ratio, namely:
- Investment analysis (analysis on payback period, NPV, IRR, and sensitivity analysis) at Appendix-12 and 13 / 14.
- Analysis and financial ratio (analysis on Break Event Point, Liquidity, ROE, ROI, Leverage, etc.) See financial attachment at

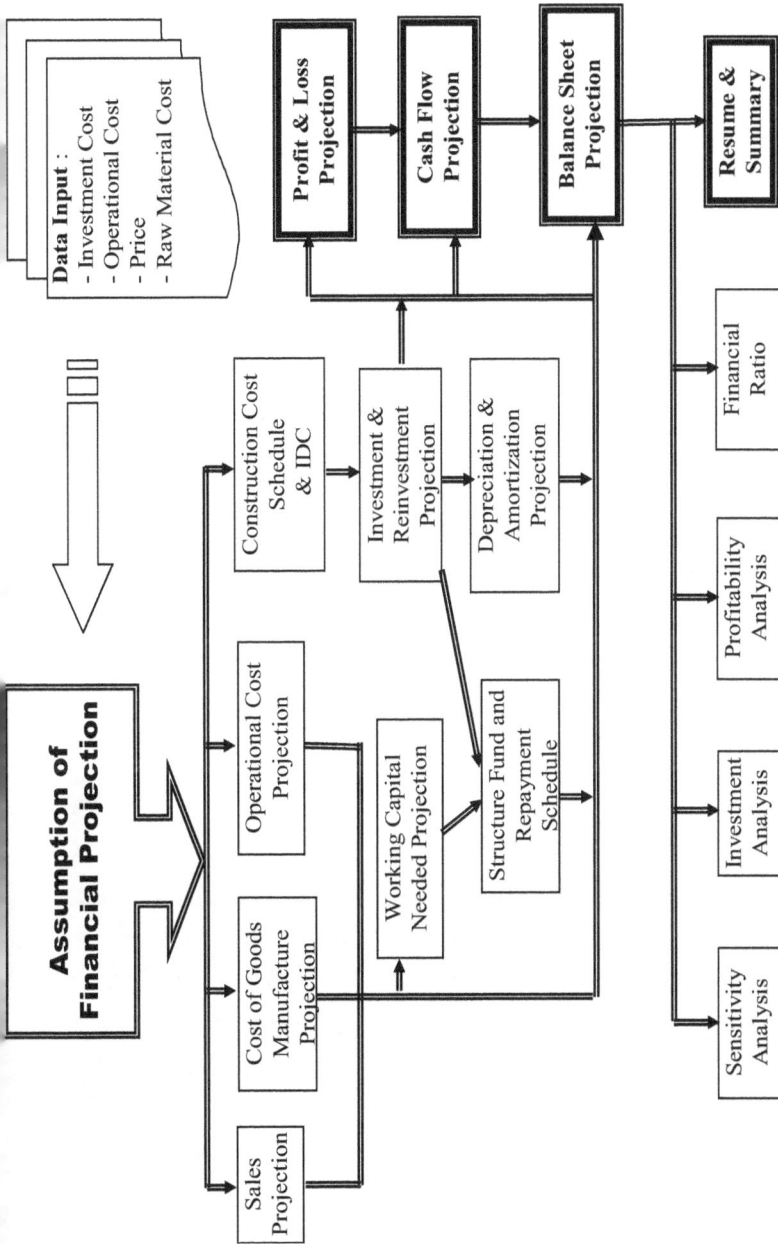

Data Input :
- Investment Cost
- Operational Cost
- Price
- Raw Material Cost

Profit & Loss Projection

Cash Flow Projection

Balance Sheet Projection

Resume & Summary

Assumption of Financial Projection

Construction Cost Schedule & IDC

Investment & Reinvestment Projection

Depreciation & Amortization Projection

Operational Cost Projection

Working Capital Needed Projection

Structure Fund and Repayment Schedule

Cost of Goods Manufacture Projection

Sales Projection

Financial Ratio

Profitability Analysis

Investment Analysis

Sensitivity Analysis

Picture - 3 Flow Chart of Financial Projection Design

Appendix-0 and 11

After having prepared complete financial projection, furtherly prepared narration (brief story) for explaining calculation results and business development plan analysis. In order that shareholders and creditor easier understand it.

The following we shall deal with the study cases that I have ever done.

The Study Case
Chemical Industries

Attention.
To know more profound technique of plan analysis you can study it from the book "**A to Z Entrepreneur In Practice**", Author Harmaizar Zaharuddin

PART TWO

STEPS OF BUSINESS PLAN ANALYSIS
(The Study Case)

PROJECT

CHEMICAL INDUSTRIES

SAMPLE OF PROPOSAL

PROJECT

CHEMICAL INDUSTRIES

"PLASTICIZER"

BUSINESS PLAN ANALYSIS

LIST OF CONTENTS

FORM - D   General & Administrative Expenses

FORM - E   Production, Raw Material Cost & Selling Price

Chapter I
Executive Summary

I.1.   Project Description

Lion Chemistries Ltd. is joint venture a company which is established by notaries deed No.......on......, 200x, in front of The Notary Public Mr. ...., in Jakarta.

The company is established for the purpose of producing the Plasticizer which is the raw materials for industries such as PVC Leather, Cable, Pipes, Shoe, Molding.

The technology to be used will be directly obtained from the Engineering, Procurement and Construction of this Plasticizer plant which will be carried out by main constructor of the .... or ....

I.2.   Share Holders

The authorized capital of the company according to the notaries deed of establishment is US$ .... (............... ....United States Dollars).

The paid-up capital at the time of establishment is US$ ....(...........................United States Dollars) or .... shares.

Shareholders according to the deed of establishment are:

1.   King Chemistries Ltd.

2.   Mistubishi & Co. Ltd.

3.   Petrokimia Co. Ltd.

Most of the licenses for conducting the business have already been obtained. Title of land ownership is under preparation or in process.

I.3.   Financial Plan

The total investment cost of Plasticizer plant is estimated to be US$ 20,418,000, including base cost and working capital for 1 years. The financing structure as follows

Equity:

- Fixed Investment	US$	4,497,000 (30 %)
- Management Fee	US$	52,000
- Commitment Fee	US$	125,000
Total Equity	US$	4,674,000

Bank loan:

- Fixed Investment Loan	US$	10,493,000 (70 %)
- Interest During Construction	US$	906,000
- Working Capital	US$	4,344,000 (100 %)
Total Loan	US$	15,743,000
Grand Total Investment	**US$**	**20,418,000**

I.4.   Legal Basis of the Company

Lion Chemistries Ltd. is a foreign investment and limited liability company established by notaries deed No. ....., on ....200x, in front of The Notary Public Mr. ...., Bachelor of Law, in Jakarta.

The licenses and references which have already been obtained by the company for operating the Plasticizer plant are as follow:

1. Business Operation License No............ issued by the Head of the Jakarta Regional Office of the Department of Trade ...., 200x... in Jakarta.

2. Company Registration Number from the Jakarta office of the Department of Trade, number .... with validity until ......, 200x, as issued on ....., 200x in Jakarta.

3. Letter of Company Domicile Number ../......./200x issued by the Head of the Village-head ...., District ...., Central Jakarta, on ...., 200x

4. Taxpayer Registration Number, ... issued by the Directorate General of Taxes, Central Jakarta Office, on ...., 200x.

5. Notification of Presidential Approval, issued by Board of Coordination of Domestic & Foreign Investments, No. ....dated ....

I.5.   Investment Proposal

The total investment cost of the Plasticizer plant is estimated to be US$ 56,932,000 including interest during construction.

Sources of funds for financing the Plasticizer plant of Lion Chemistries Ltd. are bank loans (long term loan) and equity.

The project financing structure as follows:

- Bank loan	US$	41,488,000
- Equity	US$	15,444,000
Total	**US$**	**56,932,000**

_____

CHAPTER II
ECONOMIC AND MARKETINGASPECTS

II.1   INTRODUCTION

The development in the industrial sector of the Indonesian economy, from 2004 to 2008, has gradually resulted in a solid growth of the industrial sector which is capable of providing an increasingly tangible contribution to the Indonesian economy. The capability for solid growth is manifested in the rapid development in year 2007 in spite of an unfavorable economic situation.

The growth of the industrial sector in 2007 reached 6.33% annually, a growth rate which surpassed the national economic growth by 3.7% per year. Comparing this to the target for the national economic growth for year 2007 which was set at 9.5%/year average, it can be seen that this target has been exceeded. The Contribution of the industrial sector in the Gross Domestic Product was 9.6% at the end of year 2004, 10.6%, at the end of year 2005, 12.5% at the end of year 2006 and the contribution had reached 18.4% at the end of year 2007.

Reaching the end of year 2007, the structure of the national industry had deepened and grown more solid as shown by the expanding investment for the deepening of the industrial structure which was for the development of the basic industries which included the Basic chemical, Machinery, Basic Metal and Electronics as well as other various industries.

The growth and development of the up-stream or basic industries, which in general are oriented towards the processing of natural and other resources into raw/intermediate materials, components and spare parts as well as capital goods, have gradually reduced the dependency of the industrial sector on imported goods. The development of the basic/primary industries has also contributed to the solidity of the national industrial structure.

At the end of year 2007, the interest to invest in the construction of basic/up-stream industrial projects was substantial and directed to both new projects as well as expansion projects in the field of aromatics, olefines, pulp for rayon, paper and the expansion of state as well as private steel mills. One of these up-stream industries is the industry to produce Plasticizer

II.2.   Analysis of Demand and Supply

At the present moment, there is are Plasticizer producers in Indonesia.such as Buana Chemical Industries Ltd. and Petrokimia Ltd.

The demand for Plasticizer mostly comes from the industry of PVC Leather, Cable, Pipes, Shoe and Molding Industries

The following table-II.1 shows the actual market supply of Plasticizer in Indonesia from 2004 to 2008 and the future projected demand of Plasticizer in Indonesia from 2009 to the year of 2016.

Table-II.1   Actual and Projection Supply of Plasticizer.

Year	Plasticizer (MTPA)
Actual	
2004	44,500
2005	46,000
2006	48,500
2007	51,000
2008	52,000
Projected	
2009	50,000
2010	60,000
2011	75,000
2012	110,000
2013	110,000
2014	140,000
2015	160,000
2016	160,000

The following table-II.2 shows the actual market demand of Plasticizer in Indonesia from 2004 to 2008 and the future projected demand of Plasticizer in Indonesia from 2009 to the year of 2015.

Table-II.2   Actual and Projection Demand of Plasticizer.

Year	Plasticizer (MTPA)
Actual	
2004	40,000
2005	45,000
2006	44,000
2007	48,000
2008	52,000
Projected	
2009	50,000
2010	56,000
2011	64,000
2012	73,000
2013	83.500
2014	93,500
2015	106,000
2016	120,000

Source : Central Bureau of Statistic (BPS).

II.3.   Import history

As it has been described that, there is no Plasticizer producers in Indonesia. However as the demand has been higher than the supply, Indonesia still has to import from several countries such as :
1 Japan
2. Taiwan
3 U. S. A
4 Australia
5 Netherlands

6 R. F. Germany

The actual growth of the amount of Plasticizer imported to Indonesia in the past few years is as follow:

Table-II.2   The Actual Growth of of Plasticizer Import

Year	Plasticizer (MTPA)
Actual	
2004	6,000
2005	6,500
2006	7,000
2007	6,250
2008	6,500
Projected	
2009	5,000
2010	3,000
2011	2,000
2012	1,000
2013	2.000
2014	1,000
2015	1,000
2016	1,000

Source: Central Bureau of Statistic (BPS).

II.4.   Projected Production

Lion Chemistries Ltd. is expected to start its production of Plasticizer in 2012. The projected production of the company until the year of 2015 is presented in the following tables:

Table-II.3   Production Sales Schedules of Plasticizer by

Lion Chemistries Ltd. for the period of 2011 - 2016.

Year	Output (MTPA)	Sales	
		Local Market (MTPA)	Export Market (MTPA)
2011	24,000	16,000	8,000
2012	27,000	17,960	9,040
2013	30,000	20,035	9,965
2014	30,000	21,239	8,761
2015	30,000	22,588	7,412
2016	30,000	24,099	5,901

II.5. Balance Between projected Demand and Supply

As explained earlier that there is no manufacturers of Plasticizer in Indonesia. The following is the progress of the projected supply and demand can be shown on table-II.4.

Table II.4   Balance Between Projected Supply and Demand of Plasticizer per-annum for the period of 2009 - 2016

Year	Supply			Demand (MTPA)	Export (MTPA)
	Domestic (MTPA)	Import (MTPA)	Total (MTPA)		
Actual					
2004	44,500	6,000	50,500	40,000	10,500
2005	46,000	6,500	52,500	45,000	7,500
2006	48,500	7,000	55.500	44,000	11,500
2007	51,000	6,250	57,250	48,000	9,250
2008	52,000	6,500	58,500	52,000	6,500
Projected					
2009	50,000	5,000	55,000	50,000	5,000
2010	60,000	3,000	63,000	56,000	7,000
2011	75,000	2,000	77,000	64,000	13,000
2012	110,000	1,000	111,000	73,000	38,000
2013	110,000	2,000	112,000	83,000	29,000
2014	140,000	1,000	141,000	93,500	47,500
2015	160,000	1,000	161,000	106,000	55,000
2016	160,000	1,000	161,000	120,000	41,000

From the above results of projection, it can be seen that the existing supply for Plasticizer is still greater than the demand. There for Lion Chemistries Ltd. will export the excess quantity.

II.6.   Price of Products

The pricing policy of the company will correlate the selling price to the production cost and strength of demand. However, Lion Chemistries Ltd. in determining its selling price shall also use "competition oriented pricing", which means that the selling price will be fixed after taking into consideration the average selling price of the competitors and the production cost calculation.

The selling price which is decided by Lion Chemistries Ltd. is as follows:

Table-II.5.   Pricing Policy for Plasticizer

Year	Plasticizer (US$/MT)
2009	1,400

The higher local price is caused by the protection from the government.

II.7.   Marketing Strategy

II.7.1. Competition

Plasticizer produced by Lion Chemistries Ltd. will face competition from the Petronika Ltd., Buana Chemical Industries Ltd. and Wahana Ltd.

II.7.2. DISTRIBUTION

Lion Chemistries Ltd. desires that its Plasticizer gets into the consumers, in a secured, fast and timely manner. To achieve this objective, a competent distribution channel is needed. The distribution channel will be as follows :

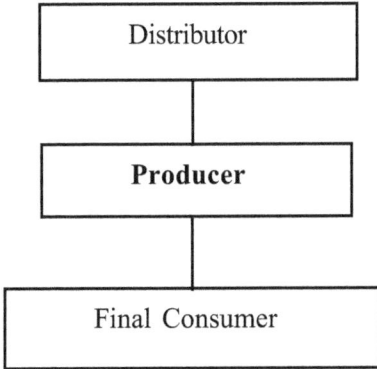

```
┌─────────────────────────────┐
│         Distributor         │
└─────────────────────────────┘
              │
┌─────────────────────────────┐
│         Producer            │
└─────────────────────────────┘
              │
┌─────────────────────────────┐
│       Final  Consumer       │
└─────────────────────────────┘
```

This type of distribution channel is the most common for distributing products to the large cities.

II.7.3. PROMOTION

The products produced by Lion Chemistries Ltd. is not yet known to the prospective consumers. Therefore, the promotion program is very important because of the competition from the imported products that are already well known to the consumers. The promotion program shall convince the consumers that the products produced by Lion Chemistries Ltd. are superior in quality so that the consumers can be persuaded to try and buy. The promotional activities that need to be done are among others:

a. Product Advertising

Lion Chemistries Ltd. will advertise its product in magazines, newspaper or other mass media. The objective is to introduce its quality product.

b. Discount

This means giving a price rebate to the customers of Plasticizer This price discount is given when beginning to sell the product to the market or on other occasions as deemed necessary by the company.

_____-

CHAPTER III
PROJECT ASPECTS

III.1. Introduction

III.1.1. General

The chemical plant is planned to produce Plasticizer is an organic chemical which is used as a raw materials in the production of PVC Leather, Cable, Pipes, Shoe and Molding Industries. Plasticizer is produced by the reaction of 2-EH and Phthalic Anhydride in 2 step reaction is Monoesterification and Diesterification.

The Plasticizer to be produced by Lion Chemistries Ltd. is of export quality and in accordance international quality standards.

Sophisticated technology and machinery are utilized for the production of Plasticizer in order to obtain a good product quality of this intermediate raw material. Therefore, expert operators are required who have the proper knowledge and skills. The machinery consist of components with interrelated functions. For this reason, the operators shall also have the competence to maintain the equipment and anticipate possible malfunctions.

Because the technology for the manufacture of Plasticizer is of foreign origin, it is essential that every local operator shall be trained for the necessary skills to operate the plant. The proprietor of the technology has indicated their agreement for training the operators. This will be achieved by training core personnel abroad (in the country originating the technology) and also by importing trainers from the originating country for training the local personnel.

III.1.2. Manufacturing of Plasticizer

The process flow diagram of Plasticizer is given in the following diagram.

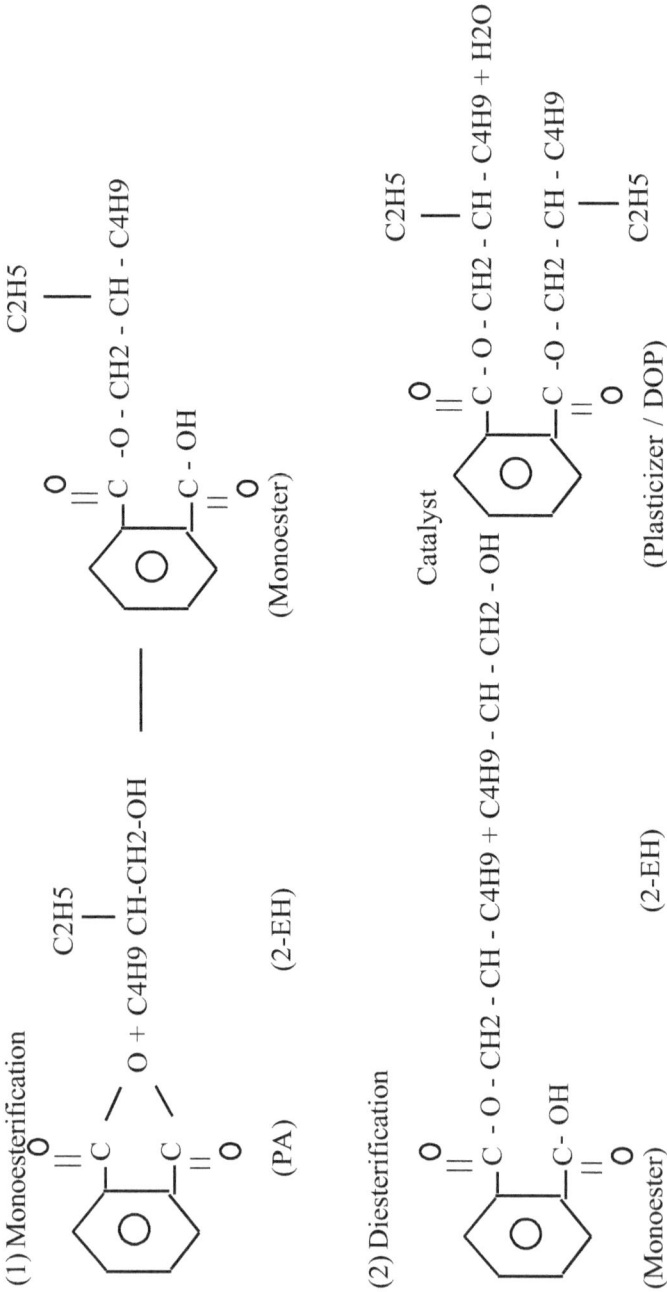

(1) Monoesterification

(PA) + (2-EH) C4H9 CH-CH2-OH / C2H5 → (Monoester)

(2) Diesterification

(Monoester) + (2-EH) C4H9 - CH - CH2 - OH / C4H9 →[Catalyst] (Plasticizer / DOP) + H2O

Process Diagram for Plasticizer Production

III.2. Plant Location

The Plasticizer plant of Lion Chemistries Ltd. is located in Bala Raja West Java, approximately 50 km from Jakarta.

The project site is about 50,000 m2 . The selection of this location was made on the basis of the following economic and technical considerations:

- Close to Merak port which will facilitate the shipment of Plasticizer and the importation of the raw materials from abroad.

- Abundant manpower can be found around the plant location and the character of the population around the plant is suitable for the quality of manpower required as they are generally hard working, tenacious and skilled workers.

- The infrastructure and facilities required by the factory are already available adjacent to the plant location.

III.3. Project Schedule

Construction of the Plasticizer plant will start in the first quarter 2009 and will be ready for use by the end second quarter 2010. The construction will be done by foreign contractor with its associated local and foreign subcontractors which will be appointed by Lion Chemistries Ltd..

The diagram project schedule can be seen in Appendix 07 or 07A.

III.4. Plant Description

III.4.1. Land

The land for the site of this project needs land improvements and cleaning with an area of 50,000 m2.

To facilitate transportation of the raw material to the plant warehouse, the company will construct an asphalted road. To beautify and improve the yard the scenery parks and ponds will be constructed in appropriate areas.

As a preventive measure for the security of the plant a sturdy fence shall be constructed around the site.

III.4.2. Production Machinery

The production machinery required by Lion Chemistries Ltd. factory for production of Plasticizer can be classified in 2 sections : ISBL AND OSBL.

ISBL (Inside Battery limit) Facilities :

30,000 MTPA of 100% Plasticizer plant. The ISBL facilities include all unit storage including product shift tanks and storage.

OSBL (Outside Battery limit) Facilities :

Electrical sub-station and motor control centre

Emergence power generation (5000 kVA MW diesel driven).

Spare part for 2 years

III.4.3. Utilities

Electricity

In order to meet the electric power requirement of the project, a generating set will be used. The requirement for electric power will be supplied by PLN.

Water

Water will mainly be required for daily use and for cooling of the machinery. The requirement for filtered water will be supplied from deep weal.

III.5. Investment Cost

The total project cost of the Plasticizer project of Lion Chemistries

Ltd. is estimated to be US$ 14,991,000, as follows :

Land Cost	US$	2,500,000
Land Improvement	US$	200,000
ISBL (Inside Battery Limit)	US$	5,600,000
OSBL (Outside Battery Limit)	US$	3,924,000
Other Facilities :		
Vehicles	US$	144,000
Tools & Office Equipment	US$	187,000
Pre-Operating Expenses :		
Technical Asst. & Training	US$	150,000
Project Management	US$	250,000
Star-up & Commissioning Cost	US$	100,000
Miscelenius	US$	135,000
Total assets	US$	14,991,000

____

CHAPTER IV
INVESTMENT AND MANAGEMENT ASPECT

IV.1.   Project Background

There is a remarkable development in Plasticizer industry during the past few years. The reason for this is the increasing demand for this chemical which is the raw material for various industries such as for PVC Leather, Cable, Pipes Shoe and Molding Industries and other products. It is estimated that by the year of 2000, the demand for Plasticizer will be 120,000 Metric Tons per-year. There is also an opportunity to export Plasticizer because this chemical is also used by other countries.

With the above mentioned background, King Chemistries Ltd. and Mitsubishi & Co., LTD will establish Lion Chemistries Ltd. as the joint venture company to produce Plasticizer

IV.2.   Share Ratio

The authorized capital of the company according to the notaries deed of establishment is US$ ....which is divided into ....shares, each with a nominal value of US$ ....

The paid-up capital at the time of establishment is US$ ...... or .... shares according to specification as follows:

1. King Chemistries Ltd : ….....shares

2. Mitsubishi & Co. Ltd : ….....shares

IV.3.   Board of director

The management team of the company consists of businessmen

who are well experienced in the conduct of various businesses. Management consists of the following:

1. The President Commissioner

2. The Commissioner first

3. The Commissioner second

4. The President Director

IV.4.   Organization

The organizational structure of the Lion Chemistries Ltd. is designed according to the functions that are required for the realization of the company's objectives.

The objective of Lion Chemistries Ltd. Are like any other well established enterprises, to secure a reasonable profit for the shareholders and to give satisfaction to all that are dealing with the company (personnel, government, distributors and consumers) and all of this without disregarding the continuity and future of the company.

Lion Chemistries Ltd. is managed by the President Director. The function of the Manager is to act as the executive of the company for planning and execution of the daily operation of the company and to be responsible to the commissioner. The function of the commissioner is to represent the shareholders in supervising the operation of the company.

In this day to day work, the President Director is assisted by 4 managers who in turn are responsible for the following departments:

1. Finance and Administration Manager

2. Production Manager

3. Marketing Manager

4. General & Adm. Manager

In order to execute these functions and objectives, the following organizational structure has been designed as follows. (See Diagram IV.1.)

The role of each Manager is to carry out the main function in the operation of the company. The managers supervise a number of staff and the executing personnel.

The duties and responsibilities of each department are as follows:

Diagram IV.1   Organization Structure Organization Structure of Lion Chemistries Ltd.

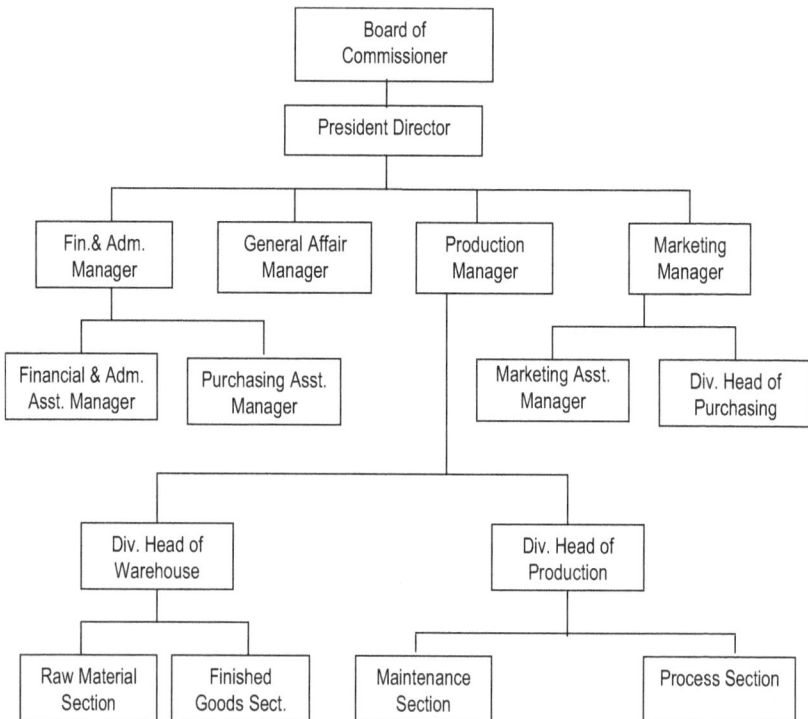

IV.4.1. General and Personal Affairs Department

The General Affairs and Personnel Department are led by a Manager. The main duties and responsibilities of the General affairs and Personnel sections are to manage and control the office operations, among others:

1. Manpower planning and personnel requirement.

2. Personnel registration.

3. Execute and coordinate the administrative tasks.

4. Manage and coordinate office operations.

IV.4.2. Finance and Administration Department

The finance and Administration Department is led by a Manager who is subordinating 2 section heads:

1. Finance Section

2. Administration and Accounting Sections

Duties and responsibilities of the Assistant Finance and Administration manager are:

1. To execute the company's bookkeeping tasks, cost accounting, analysis of financial reports in order to obtain efficiency and good profitability.

2. To execute purchasing, payments and collections as well as other company business involving financial transactions.

3. To plan, implement and prepare the company's budget and cash flow.

4. To pay salaries and look after the welfare of the personnel.

IV.4.3.　Production/Technical department

The production department is led by a Manager who supervises 4 sections:

1. Production Planning & Inventory Control

2. Factory Administrative section

3. Production Section

4. Quality Control & Assurance Section

each of these sections is led by a manager as the section head. The duties and responsibilities of the production department are among others:

1. To execute tasks that are directly connected to the production of Plasticizer

2. To carry out control for each step of the production process.

3. To test each production batch according to the applicable technical requirements.

4. To be responsible for the smooth operation of the plant's machinery and equipment.

5. To carry out activities relating to logistics (warehousing and procurement)

IV.4.4.　Sales/marketing Department

The sales/marketing department is led by a manager who is assisted by 2 section heads:

1. Purchasing section

2. Marketing section

The duties and responsibilities of the sales/marketing department are among others:

1. To know the market and obtain information about the market.

2. To define potential markets and make prediction about their absorption capacity.

3. To accept orders from consumers.

4. To carry out promotion of the company's products.

5. To carry out the pricing policies as established by the company.

6. To sell products to local and export markets.

IV.5. Company Management

An important component of the organization is the management, which is the manner in which the company's and the environmental resources are processed and utilized for the operation of the company. The management shall follow modern management principles such as planning, organization, implementation and control as far as possible.

Management aspects that need to be headed are among others:

IV.5.1. Goods Raw Material Management

which consists of:

1. Selection of raw materials and auxiliary materials which as far as possible be obtained from domestic sources and located close to the factory location.

2. Utilization of efficient and economic means of transport.

3. Careful and systematic handling and storage of raw materials.

IV.5.2. Production Management

which consists of:

1. Selection of raw materials and auxiliary materials with standard quality according to the company specified standards and com-

petitive in quality.

2. Selection of good quality machinery in order to obtain an economical ratio of purchase price and output produced.

3. Utilization of an efficient production system by means of, among others, a well planned factory and machinery lay-out.

4. Establishment of a system to control the quality of production by implementing appropriate and strict quality control systems.

5. Complying to all government regulations that are applicable to the company.

IV.5.3. Personnel Management

which consists of:

1. Ascertaining the number and qualification of personnel according to their functions and duties in their respective fields.

2. As far as possible personnel shall be recruited from around the factory location. This has the advantage of reducing recruitment costs and providing employment (especially for laborers) to the neighboring population.

3. Providing training and education to the personnel as required by their respective duties and functions in order to facilitate operations and strengthen professionalism.

4. Developing personnel's morale and material welfare to increase their motivation and diligence.

IV.5.4. Marketing management

consisting of:

1. Selection of a market segment after first conducting a market survey in order to find out about the market potential and consumer preferences.

2. Making short of possible the distribution chain if possible in order to reduce cost and improve efficiency.

3. Selling price should be determined by taking in consideration costs, product characteristics (whether product is competitive or not) and also taking into account competition from other companies.

IV.6. Investment Detail

This investor detail of the construction of Plasticizer of Lion Chemistries Ltd. as follows:

1. King Chemistries Ltd.

2. Mitsubishi & Co., LTD

3. Tirta Chemistries Ltd

Is an Indonesia-registered company established in 200x with the corporate objective to focus on resource-based industries. It has interests in building materials, coal mining, agribusiness and petrochemicals. Associated companies include chip Semen Tirta Ltd, a publicly listed company and Indonesia's second largest cement and concrete group. This company operate a 3 million ton per annum cement plant and hopes to expand by another 1 million tons. Other interests of Tirta Ltd. are energy-related including coal mining, coal bulk handling, power supply and oil storage. lately it has embarked on three major petrochemical project commercial, transport and international trading expertise.

4. Petrokimia Ltd.

Petrokimia Ltd (Persero) is a state owned company under the laws of the republic of Indonesia, having at principal office at Street: Duck, Jakarta, Indonesia.

The main line of business of the company is producing of various kinds of fertilizer products such as ammonium sulphate, urea, TSP, and chemical product such as sulphuric acid, phosphoric acid, cement retarder and aluminum fluoride.

CHAPTER V
FINANCIAL ASPECTS

V.1.   Fixed Assets

The total investment cost of the Plasticizer project of Lion Chemistries Ltd. is estimated to be US$ 16,073,000 as follows:

Land:

Land Cost	US$	2,500,000
Land Improvement	US$	200,000
Construction:		
ISBL	US$	5,600,000
OSBL (Outside Battery Limit)	US$	3,924,000
Other Facilities:		
Vehicles	US$	144,000
Tools & Office Equipment	US$	187,000
Pre-Operating Expenses:		
Technical Asst. & Training	US$	150,000
Project Management	US$	250,000
Star-up & Commissioning Cost	US$	100,000
Miscelenius	US$	135,000
Others:		
I D C	US$	905,000
Management Fee	US$	53,000
Commitment Fee	US$	124,000
Total Assets	US$	16,073,000

Structure of funds:

The investment cost is planned to be financed by bank loan and equity.

Financing structure is as follows:

Bank loan:
- Investment	US$	10,493,000 (70%)
- I. D. C.	US$	906,000

Equity:
- Investment cost	US$	4,497,000 (30%)
- Management Fee	US$	52,000
- Commitment Fee	US$	125,000
Total Investment Cost	US$	16,073,000

V.2. Re-Investment

Re- investment cost is estimated as follows:

Vvehicles 6th year	US$	232,000
Tools & Office Equipment 6th year	US$	302,000
Total re-investment	US$	534,000

V.3.   Working Capital

The working capital is required for 2 years as follows:

Year 1 US$ 4,344,000

V.4.   Sources of Funds

The investment cost needed is planned to be financed by banks and equity. The working capital needed is planned to be financed by banks.

V.5.   Financial Assumption

The following assumptions have been made in preparing this financial projection :

V.5.1.   Working Days

It is assumed that the plant is running on at 330 working days per year.

V.5.2.   Shifts and Working Hours

The plant will operate 24 hours a day (i.e. 3 shifts per-day)

V.5.3.   Production Capacity

After the construction of Plasticizer the plant which will be completed at the end of forth quarter of 2011, will have output of 2,400 MTPA in 2012. Full capacity will be achieved in the third year at 30,000 MTPA.

V.5.4.   Types of product

The products of the plant are Plasticizer which is used as raw materials for the production of the followings:

- PVC Calendaring
- Compounding of synthetic leather
- Coating of electrical cable & wire
- Sports shoes component
- and etc.

V.5.5.   Raw Materials Cost and Selling Price

Raw Materials Cost:

The purchasing of raw materials is located. Estimated raw materials cost per-MT in 2010 is as follows:

Product (Plasticizer) for local market:

- 2-EH	US$	670 / mt
- PA	US$	450 / mt
Total	US$	1,120 / mt

Product(Plasticizer) for import market:

- 2-EH	US$	600 / mt
- PA	US$	360 / mt
Total	US$	960 / mt

Selling Price:

The average selling price of products in 2010 is as follows :

Plasticizer US$ 1,400 / mt

V.5.6. Depreciation and Maintenance

Depreciation is calculated using the Straight Line Method.

The useful life of the assets cost are as follows:

V.5.7. Sales and Cost Price Escalation and Unit of Calculation

No	Description	Depreciation & Useful Life
I	**Depreciation:**	
1	I.S.B.L.	10 year
2	O.S.B.L.	10 year
3	Factory Vehicle	5 year
4	Land Improvement	10 year
5	Office Vehicle & Equipment	5 year
II	**Pre-Operating:**	
1	IDC	5 year
2	Management Fee	5 year
3	Commitment Fee	5year

Sales and cost price escalation are as follows:

Re-Investment cost	5.00%
Selling price escalation	2.50%
Raw materials cost escalation	2.50%

Cost/Expenses escalation:

- Factory Overhead cost	5.00%
- Selling Expenses	2.50%
- General Administrative Expenses	5.00%
- Labor Cost	10.00%

Calculations are made in US$ and any differences arising from these are due to rounding off.

V.5.8. Taxes

Income tax is calculated according to the tax regulation, as follows:

Profit	Tax
up to US$ 1,000	15 %
US$ 1000 up to US$ 5000,	25 %
US$ 5000 <	35 %

Exchange rate 1 US$ = Rp 10,000
This analysis use average tax 30%
Value Added Tax (VAT) is not considered.

V.5.9.   Accounts Payable and Receivable

Credit term of accounts payable and receivable are assumed to be:

1. Accounts payable/Purchases:

    - Import   0.0 month

    - local   2.0 month

2. Accounts receivable/Sales:

    - Export   0.0   month

    - Local   2.0   month

V.5.10. Inventory

Raw materials inventory is determined for 1 months.

Goods in process inventory is determined for 0.03 month.

Finished goods inventory is determined for 0.5 month.

Cash requirement is determined for 3 months.

V.5.11. Insurance

Insurance premium for the plant and office comprises of :

- Insurance premium for ISBL (Inside Battery Limit) is at 0.37% of the new procurement costs.

- Insurance premium for OSBL (Outside Battery Limit) is at 0.37% of the new procurement costs.

- Insurance premium for motor vehicles is at 2.50% of the new procurement costs.

- Personnel insurance is at 1.50% of the personnel costs.

V.5.12. Cost of Money

- Interest rate for old investment loan is 9.00 % per-year.

- Interest rate for working capital loan is 10.00 % per-year.

- Foreign exchange losses is 5.00 % per-year.

V.5.13. Interest During Construction (IDC)

Interest during construction is calculated from the S-curve to be 8.63% of the loans required during the construction period and is obtained by multiplying the construction period with the interest rate for the investment loans.

V.5.14.   Grace Period

The grace period required for the repayment of the investment loan facility to bank is projected for approximately 1.5 years, start from the beginning construction.

V.5.15.   Costs & Operating Expenses

The breakdown of yearly Production costs, selling expenses, general and administrative expenses can be seen in Appendix-10.

V.6.   Financial Projections

> The narration of financial projection below is made after **CALCULATION of FINANCIAL PROJECTION has** been made completely. See Appendix-Financial Projection.

V.6.1.   Re-Investment Schedule

It is expected that by the end fourth quarter of 1995 the Plasticizer project will be ready for commercial production.

From second year to tenth year there will be re-investment on fixed assets, which useful life have been fully depreciated, such as ; Factory Vehicles, Office & Equipment.

The re-investment schedule can be seen in Appendix-08.

V.6.2.   Depreciation and Maintenance Schedule

The fixed assets are depreciated within 5 to 10 years by using Straight Line Depreciation Method.

The amount of depreciation for one year production at normal plant capacity in the third year is shown in the following table:

Third year:

No	Description	Depreciation (in US$)
I	**Depreciation:**	
1	I.S.B.L.	200,000
2	O.S.B.L.	560,000
3	Vehicles	392,000
4	Land Improvement	28,000
5	Tool & Office Equipment	36,000
II	**Amortization:**	
1	IDC	217,000
2	Management & Commit. Fee	127,00

Please refer to Appendix-09.

V.6.3. Schedule of Cash Requirement

Cash requirement is the total cash requirement to support the day to day business operation.

Detail in Appendix-10

V.6.4. Cost of Goods Sold

The cost of goods sold is determined by the fluctuation of costs. The projection for cost of goods sold is shown in Appendix-04.

The first year total cost of goods sold is US$ 27,803,000. Normal capacity (100%) will be achieved in the third year and the cost of goods sold is US$ 41,417,000.

V.6.5. Working Capital Requirement

In this study, working capital means the difference between current assets and current liabilities. The working capital is needed in the first year is estimated to be US$ 4,344,000.

The breakdown of the working capital requirement is shown in Appendix-11

V.6.6.   Investment Loan Disbursements and Repayments

The principal of the investment loans will be fully repaid by the fifth year

The schedule for total investment loan repayment will be as follows:

Year	Fixed Investment Loan (US$)	Working Capital Loan (US$)
year 1	500	500
year 2	1,500	500
year 3	2,000	1,000
year 4	2,000	1,000
year 5	2,000	1,000
year 6	3,399	344
Total	**11,399**	**4,344**

Please refer to Appendix-06 for the loan disbursement and repayment schedule.

V.6.7.   Profit and Loss Projection

The first year projection, the company will a profit of US$ 623,000. In the second year the company will a profit of US$ 1,514,000. For the years after, please refer to Appendix-03.

V.6.8.   Cash Flow Projection

Appendix-02 exhibits the in-flows of fund from operation (sales revenues) and also from loan, as well as out-flows for operational costs & loan repayment.

V.6.9.   Production and Sales Projections

From the production and sales projection as shown in Appendix-05 it reflects that some finish products are left over for safety stock.

The sales volume of products in the first year is 22,940 MTPA with net sales revenue of US$ 32,116,000.

In the second year sales volume of products increases to 26,868,000 MTPA. In fourth year the sales achieves maximum capacity of 30,000 MTPA with net sales revenue of US$ 48,620,000.

V.6.10. Balance Sheet Projection

The purpose of the balance sheet is to present information about the financial position of the company in the form of assets, loan and capital. The balance sheet is prepared at the end of every production year.

The financial position of the company is determined by the analysis of its liquidity, rentability and solvability, which reflect that the financial position of the company improve from year to year.

V.6.11. Internal Rate of Return (IRR)

The IRR can be defined as the interest rate at which the present value of future (expected) proceeds is equal to the present value of the capital outlays.

The IRR is acceptable when it is larger than the prevailing bank interest rate. In the internal rate of return analysis of

Lion Chemistries Ltd., it is found that the IRR on EBIT based on net profit is 24.68%. This shows that it is feasible to utilize the funds for this project.

The IRR projections are shown in Appendix-13.

V.6.12. Payback Period

The payback period is the period needed to recover the investment by mean of the proceeds (net profit after tax plus depreciation).

The payback period of the Lion Chemistries Ltd. project is approximately 4 years.

The payback period can be seen in Appendix-12

V.7.   Financial Ratio Analysis

V.7.1.   Liquidity

The ability of Lion Chemistries Ltd. to meet its current obligations is as follows :

Year	Liquidity
Year-1	119.38%
Year-2	137.55%
Year-3	160.15%
Year-4	193.53%
Year-5	235.52%
Year-6	242.77%

Further details can be seen in Appendix-13

V.7.2.   Profitability

The ability of Lion Chemistries Ltd. to generate profits from the assets invested can be measured by the Rate of Return on Investment (ROI) and the Rate of Return on Equity (ROE).

The ROI and ROE of Lion Chemistries Ltd. are as follows :

Year	ROI	ROE
Year-1	9.50%	11.76%
Year-2	14.14%	22.23%
Year-3	17.83%	25.50%
Year-4	18.36%	22.17%
Year-5	18.30%	19.30%
Year-6	19.49%	17.96%

ROI and ROE of the following years can be seen in Appendix-13.

V.7.3.   Solvability

The ability of the company to meet all its debts, both short as well as long term loans when the company is liquidated can be measured by analyzing its solvability. Solvability can be measured by using the debt ratio and the long term debt to capitalization ratio.

Debt ratio and long term debt to capitalization ratio of Lion Chemistries Ltd. are as follows :

Year	Debt to Equity Ratio	Long Term debt to Capitalization
Year-0	70.92%	70.92%
Year-1	78.72%	67.29%
Year-2	72.64%	57.98%
Year-3	63.59%	44.73%
Year-4	52.96%	31.49%
Year-5	42.02%	18.93%
Year-6	28.72%	0%
Year-7		

The debt ratio of the company reduces every year because the outstanding debt is diminishing where as the total assets are increasing.

The ratio of long term debt to capitalization shows the spending policy of the company. It can be seen that this ratio is gradually decreasing such that in the ninth year the ratio is 0%. The solvability ratio for other years can be seen in Appendix-0.

V.7.4.   Sensitivity Analysis

To find out about the effect of changes in the assumptions of investment cost, selling price, production cost, raw materials cost and production quantity on the IRR, a sensitivity analysis can be performed.

This analysis is presented by applying the following assumptions:

1. Selling price changes while the, production cost, raw materials, investment cost and production quantity are assumed constant. This analysis is started by assuming that the selling price decreases 5.00% and production cost, raw materials cost, investment cost and production quantity remains the same. This is repeated with selling price increasing 7.00% and production cost, raw materials cost, investment cost and production quantity remaining constant.

2. Raw materials cost changes while the selling price, production cost, investment cost and production quantity is assumed constant. This analysis is started by assuming that the raw materials cost decreases 5.00% and the selling price, raw materials cost, investment cost and production quantity remains the same. This is repeated with the raw materials cost increasing 7.00% and the selling price, production cost, investment cost and production quantity remaining constant.

3. Production cost changes while the, selling price, raw materials cost, investment cost and production quantity are assumed constant. This analysis is started by assuming that the production cost decreases 5,00 % and the, selling price, raw materials cost, investment cost and production quantity remains the same. This is repeated with the production cost increasing 7.00% and the selling price raw materials cost, investment cost and production quantity remaining constant.

4. Investment cost change while the, selling price, production cost, raw materials and production quantity are assumed constant. This analysis is started by assuming that the investment cost decreases 5.00% and selling price, production cost, raw materials cost and production quantity remains the same. This is repeated with selling price increasing 7% and selling price, production cost, raw materials cost and production quantity remaining constant.

5. Production quantity changes while the, Selling price, production cost, raw materials and investment cost are assumed constant. This analysis is started by assuming that the production quantity is 80.00% until 100.00% and Selling price, production cost, raw materials and investment cost remaining constant.

- The analysis shows that the decrease of the selling price by **5.00%** will result in an IRR that is below the cost of capital for this project which is assumed at around 9.00% or at **6.29%**. Further analysis shows that the increasing of the selling price by 5.00% increase the IRR to 36.51%. From this, it can be seen that the IRR is enough sensitive to changes in selling price.

- The analysis shows that the Increase of the production cost by 5,00% will result in an IRR that is still above the cost of capital for this project which is assumed at around 9% or at 20.88%. Further analysis shows that the decrease of the production cost by 5.00% will decrease the IRR to 26.85%. From this, it can be seen that the IRR is not sensitive to changes in production cost.

- The analysis shows that the increase of the raw materials cost by 5,00% will result in an IRR that is below the cost of capital for this project which is assumed at around 9.00% or at 9.80%. Further analysis shows that the decrease of the raw materials cost by 5.00% will increase the IRR to 34.43%.

- The analysis shows that the Increase of the investment cost by 5,00% will result in an IRR that is still above the cost of capital for this project which is assumed at around 9% or at 23.35%. Further analysis shows that the decrease of the investment cost by 5.00% will the IRR to 26.10%. From this, it can be seen that the IRR is not sensitive to changes in production cost.

- The analysis show is started by assuming that the production quantity is **75.00%** will result in an IRR that is below the cost of capital for this project which is assumed at around

9.00% or at **7.30%**. if the production quantity is started to above 80.00% will increase in the IRR is above the cost of capital.

In the sensitivity analysis, the most sensitive variable is the decrease of salling price and decrease production Quantity. But, because of the rate of the sales price decrease and production Quantity are quite large, so the project of Lion Chemistries Ltd. is proper to be run further. For more details, see in the Appendix-14.

_____

FINANCIAL PROJECTION

Business Plan Analysis

FORM
&
APPENDIX

NEW STEEL PROFILE LTD.

MAIN MENU
FINANCIAL PROJECTION

MENU:

FORM - A	Investment Cost
FORM - B	Factory Overhead Cost
FORM - C	Selling Expenses
FORM - D	General & Administrative Expenses
FORM - E	Production Capacity & Selling Price
FORM - F	Raw Materials Cost
APPENDIX-0	Summary
APPENDIX-1	Projected Balance Sheet
APPENDIX-2	Cash Flow Projection
APPENDIX-3	Profit & Loss Projection
APPENDIX-4	Cost of Goods Sold
APPENDIX-5	Production, Sales and Collection Schedule
APPENDIX-6	Structure of Funds, Loan disbursement and Repayment Schedule
APPENDIX-7	Draw Down of Project Cost Schedule
APPENDIX-7A	Interest During Construction (IDC)
APPENDIX-8	Investment and Reinvestment Schedule
APPENDIX-9	Depreciation and Maintenance Schedule
APPENDIX-10	Cash Requirement for Operation Expenses
APPENDIX-11	Estimated Working Capital Needed
APPENDIX-12	Financial Ratio
APPENDIX-13	Interest Rate Of Return
APPENDIX-14	Sensitivity Analysis

FORM - A
CHEMICAL INDUSTRIES Ltd.
INVESTMENT COST   IN 000 US$

NO.	DESCRIPTION	VOLUME	UNIT	PRICE PER-UNIT	TOTAL PRICE
B I	LAND COST				
1	LAND COST	1	LS	2,500.00	2,500.00
2	LAND IMPROVEMENT COST	1	LS	2,000.00	2,000.00
					4,500.00
II	CONSTRUCTION :				
2	ISBL (Inside Battery Limit)				
	MACHINERIES	1.00	LS	5,000.00	5,000.00
	CONSTRUCTION	1.00	LS	600.00	600.00
					5,600.00
3	OSBL (Outside Battery Limit)				
	UTILITIES, STORAGE	1.00	LS	3,700.00	3,700.00
	Spare part for 2 year on ISBL	4.00%	LS	5,600.00	224.00
					3,924.00
4	VEHICLES				
	PLANT DIRECTOR	1	UNIT	34.09	34.09
	MANAGER'S VEHICLES	3	UNIT	18.18	54.54
	MINIBUS	2	UNIT	13.64	27.27
	FORKLIFTS	1	UNIT	22.73	22.73
	MOTOR CARS	3	UNIT	1.82	5.45
					144.09
5	TOOLS & OFFICE EQUIPMENT				
	FURNITURE & FIXTURE	3.00	LS	34.09	102.27
	TOOLS, OFFICE EQUIPMENT	3.00	LS	22.73	68.18
	PHONE (2 LINE), FAXCIMILE	2.00	LS	4.55	9.09
	AIR CONDITIONER 1 PK	5.00	UNIT	1.59	7.95
					187.49
B	PRE-OPERATION EXPENSES				
	TECHNICAL ASST. & TRAINING	1	LS	150.00	150.00
	PROJECT MANAGEMENT COST	1	LS	250.00	250.00
	STAR-UP & COMMISSIONING	1	LS	100.00	100.00
	OTHERS	1	LS	135.00	135.00
					635.00
C	OTHERS:				
	I. D. C.	8.63%			905.53
	MANAGEMENT FEE	0.50%			52.47
	COMMITMENT FEE	0.50%			124.79
					1,082.79
		Grand Total Investasi			16,073.36

FORM - B
CHEMICAL INDUSTRIES Ltd.
FACTORY OVERHEAD COST   IN 000 US

NO.	DESCRIPTION	VOLUME	UNIT	PRICE PER-UNIT	TOTAL PRICE
1	DIRECT LABOUR COST				
	SUPERVISOR	2	Person	4.40	8.80
	OPERATOR	42	Person	2.80	117.60
	MAINTENANCE	2	Person	4.40	8.80
	FORKLIFT DRIVERS	2	Person	2.55	5.09
	SECURITIES	6	Person	2.55	15.27
					155.56
2	LABOUR COST				
	PLANT GENERAL MANAGER	1	Person	130.00	130.00
	MANAGERS	3	Person	50.00	150.00
	ASS. MANAGERS	3	Person	20.00	60.00
	DISCIPLINE ENGINEER	3	Person	10.00	30.00
	SUPERVISOR	9	Person	4.40	39.60
	STAFF	8	Person	2.00	16.00
	OPERATOR	29	Person	1.60	46.40
					472.00
3	FACTORY OVERHEAD				
	CONSUMMABLE	1	LS	35.91	35.91
	WATER	1	LS	23.40	23.40
	CHEMICAL	1	LS	23.94	23.94
	TRANSPORTATION	1	LS	23.94	23.94
	LEASE FOR LAND	1	LS	100.00	100.00
	PHONE, WATER & LIGHT	1	LS	50.00	50.00
	MISCELLANEOUS	1	LS	25.00	25.00
		1	LS		
					282.19
4	INSURANCE				
	ISBL	0.37%	%	5,600.00	20.72
	OSBL	0.37%	%	3,924.00	14.52
	VEHICLES	2.50%	%	144.09	3.60
	TOOLS & OFFICE EQUIPMENT	1.50%	%	187.49	2.81
	INS. LABOURS	1.50%	%	627.56	9.41
					51.07
					333.26

FORM - C
CHEMICAL INDUSTRIES Ltd.
SELLING EXPENSES   IN 000 US$

NO.	DESCRIPTION	VOLUME	UNIT	PRICE PER-UNIT	TOTAL PRICE
1	SALARIES & OTHERS				
	MARKETING DIRECTOR	1	Person	130.00	130.00
	MARKETING MANAGER	1	Person	40.00	40.00
	ASS. MARKETING MANAGER	3	Person	10.00	30.00
	MARKETING STAFF	4	Person	4.40	17.60
	SECRETARIES	2	Person	2.00	4.00
					221.60
2	SELLING EXPENSES				
	OFFICE STATIONERIES	1.00	LS	13.30	13.30
	PHONE, WATER & LIGHT	1.00	LS	66.50	66.50
	LABOUR INSURANCE	1.50%	%	221.60	3.32
	OFFICE RENTAL	200.00	M2	0.24	48.00
	MEDICAL ALLOWANCES	2.50%	%	221.60	5.54
	OTHERS	1.00	LS	22.00	22.00
					158.66
					380.26

FORM - D
CHEMICAL INDUSTRIES Ltd.
GENERAL & ADMINISTRATIVE EXPENSES   IN 000 US$

NO.	DESCRIPTION	VOL	UNIT	PRICE PER-UN	TOTAL PRICE
1	SALARIES	67			
	DIRECTOR	2	Person	130.00	260.00
	MANAGERS	2	Person	50.00	100.00
	ASS. MANAGERS	2	Person	20.00	40.00
	SECRETARIES	6	Person	10.00	60.00
	OPERATORS	10	Person	2.80	28.00
	ADMIN	30	Person	2.00	60.00
	GENERAL	15	Person	1.60	24.00
					572.00
2	OFFICE COST				
	OFFICE RENTAL	200.00	M2	2.00	400.00
	PHONE, WATER & LIGHT	1.00	LS	35.91	35.91
	TRANSPORTATION	1.00	LS	53.20	53.20
	OFFICE SUPPLIES	1.00	LS	33.25	33.25
	OFFICE EXPENSES	1.00	LS	33.25	33.25
	OTHERS	1.00	LS	10.00	10.00
					565.61
3	PROSPERITY FUND				
	MEDICAL ALLOWANCE	2.00%	%	572.00	11.44
	INSURANCE LABOUR	2.00%	%	572.00	11.44
	INSURANCE VEHICLES	2.50%	%	572.00	14.30
	OTHERS	1.00	LS	50.00	50.00
					87.18

FORM - E

CHEMICAL INDUSTRIES Ltd.

PRODUTION, RAW MATERIALS COST & SELLING PRICE   IN US$

NO.	DESCRI	VOLUME	UNIT	PRICE US$/MT
1 PRODUCTION CAPACITY:				
	Plasticizer	30000	MT/YEAR	1,400.00

FORM - F

CHEMICAL INDUSTRIES Ltd.

RAW MATERIALS COST   IN US$

NO.	DESCRI	Import Duty	Volume	Unit	US$/MT	Total Cost
1 RAW MATERIALS :						
	- 2 EH		1.00	US$/MT	670.00	670.00
	Phthalic Anhydride		1.00	US$/MT	450.00	450.00
					T O T A I	1,120.00

APPENDIX-0
CHEMICAL INDUSTRIES Ltd.
SUMMARY & ASSUMPTION

Investment Portion:				Sales Price (US$/MT):		Mark-up Cost:	
Bank Loan:				Plasticizer	1400	Reinvestment Cost	10.00%
- Investmet	US$	10,493	70.00%	Raw Material (US$/MT):		Sales Price	5.00%
- Interest During Constr.	US$	906	100%	PA + 2 EH	1,120	Raw Material Cost	5.00%
- Working Capital	US$	4,344	100%	Normal Capacity (MTPA):		Other Cost:	
Equity:				Plasticizer	30,000	- Factory Overhead	10.00%
- Investment	US$	4,497	30.00%	Interest Rate:		- Selling Expenses	10.00%
- Management Fee	US$	52	100%	- Investment Loan	9.00%	- General Adm. Exp.	10.00%
- Commitment Fee	US$	125	100%	- Working Capital loa	10.00%	- Labor Cost	15.00%
Total	US$	20,418					

Working Capital Turnover:			Accounts Receivable:		Accounts Payable:	
Raw Material	1.00	Month	- Export	Month	- Import	Month
Goods in Process	0.03	Month	- Local	2 Month	- Local	2 Month
Finished Goods	0.50	Month				
Cash Requirement	3.00	Month	IRR	24.68%		

Continue of APPENDIX-0

Ratios:	YEAR 0	YEAR 1	YEAR 2	YEAR 3	YEAR 4	YEAR 5	YEAR 6
Gross profit (% to sales)		13.43%	14.34%	14.85%	14.82%	14.69%	14.46%
Net operating income (% to sales)		7.36%	8.91%	9.71%	9.43%	9.00%	9.05%
Net income after tax (% to sales)		1.94%	3.83%	5.06%	5.36%	5.50%	5.94%
Raw Materials cost to sales		80.00%	80.00%	80.00%	80.00%	80.00%	80.00%
Assets turnover (sales on assets)		129.01%	158.64%	183.58%	194.70%	203.35%	215.38%
R.O.I. (Ebit on Assets)		9.50%	14.14%	17.83%	18.36%	18.30%	19.49%
R.O.E. (Ebit on Equity)		11.76%	22.23%	25.50%	22.17%	19.30%	17.96%
Payback Period (YEAR)	(16,073)	(12,414)	(7,981)	(2,939)	2,091	7,043	11,253
Current Assets on total Assets		41.71%	47.99%	54.66%	60.66%	67.09%	69.72%
Liquidity		119.38%	137.55%	160.15%	193.53%	235.52%	242.77%
Equity on Assets		21.28%	27.36%	36.41%	47.04%	57.98%	71.28%
Debt to Equity		369.93%	265.50%	174.67%	112.60%	72.49%	40.29%
Debt to total assets	70.92%	78.72%	72.64%	63.59%	52.96%	42.02%	28.72%
Capitalization	70.92%	67.29%	57.98%	44.73%	31.49%	18.93%	

APPENDIX-1
CHEMICAL INDUSTRIES Ltd.
PROJECTED BALANCE SHEET

IN 000 US$

ITEMS	Year 0	Year 1	Year 2	Year 3	Year 4	Year 5	Year 6
ASSETS :							
CURRENT ASSETS:							
CASH		1,454	1,159	1,147	1,899	2,923	2,724
ACCOUNTS RECEIVABLE		5,353	6,583	7,683	8,103	8,509	8,934
RAW MATERIALS		2,240	2,646	3,087	3,241	3,403	3,574
GOODS IN PROCESS		73	85	99	104	109	115
FINISHED GOODS		1,264	1,475	1,709	1,800	1,899	2,005
TOTAL CURRENT ASSETS		10,383	11,947	13,725	15,148	16,843	17,351
FIXED ASSETS :							
INVESTMENT	14,356	14,356	14,356	14,356	14,356	14,356	14,890
ACCUMULATED DEPRECIATION		(1,219)	(2,437)	(3,656)	(4,875)	(6,094)	(7,353)
NET FIXED ASSETS	14,356	13,137	11,918	10,699	9,481	8,262	7,537
OTHER ASSETS :							
PREOP. & DEFERRED CHARGES	1,718	1,718	1,718	1,718	1,718	1,718	1,718
ACCUMULATION AMORTIZATION		(344)	(687)	(1,031)	(1,374)	(1,718)	(1,718)
NET OTHER ASSETS	1,718	1,374	1,031	687	344		
TOTAL ASSETS	16,073	24,894	24,896	25,111	24,972	25,105	24,888

Continue of APPENDIX-1

IN 000 US$

ITEMS	Year 0	Year 1	Year 2	Year 3	Year 4	Year 5	Year 6
LIABIL. AND S. HOLDERS' EQUITY							
CURRENT LIABILITIES :							
SHORT TERM LOAN		3,844	3,344	2,344	1,344	344	
ACCOUNTS PAYABLE		4,853	5,341	6,225	6,483	6,807	7,147
TOTAL CURRENT LIABILITIES		8,698	8,685	8,570	7,827	7,151	7,147
LONG TERM LOAN	11,399	10,899	9,399	7,399	5,399	3,399	
SHARE HOLDERS' EQUITY							
EQUITY	4,674	4,674	4,674	4,674	4,674	4,674	4,674
RETAINED EARNINGS		623	2,137	4,468	7,072	9,880	13,066
TOTAL SHARE HOLDERS' EQUITY	4,674	5,297	6,812	9,142	11,746	14,555	17,741
TOTAL LIAB. & EQUITY	16,073	24,894	24,896	25,111	24,972	25,105	24,888

APPENDIX-2
CHEMICAL INDUSTRIES Ltd.
CASH FLOW PROJECTION

IN 000 US$

ITEMS	Year 0	Year 1	Year 2	Year 3	Year 4	Year 5	Year 6
CASH IN-FLOWS FROM OPERATION		26,763	38,265	45,000	48,200	50,646	53,178
A/R COLLECTION		26,763	38,265	45,000	48,200	50,646	53,178
CASH OUT-FLOWS FROM OPERATION		26,912	34,555	39,864	42,468	44,837	47,436
PURCHASES		24,267	31,558	36,468	38,639	40,517	42,543
DIRECT LABOUR COST		156	179	206	237	272	313
FACTORY OVERHEAD COST		918	1,049	1,199	1,350	1,521	1,731
GENERAL & ADM. EXP.		1,192	1,339	1,506	1,695	1,908	2,148
SELLING EXPENSES		380	429	485	548	620	701
NET CASH OPERATING		(149)	3,710	5,136	5,732	5,809	5,742
TOTAL OTHER IN-FLOWS	15,168	4,344					
EQUITY	4,674						
LOAN : - LONG TERM LOAN :	10,493						
- SHORT TERM LOAN		4,344					

APPENDIX-2

IN 000 US$

ITEMS	Year 0	Year 1	Year 2	Year 3	Year 4	Year 5	Year 6
TOTAL OTHER OUT-FLOWS	15,168	267	649	999	1,116	1,204	1,899
INVESTMENT	14,991						
MGT & COMT FEE	177						534
INCOME TAX		267	649	999	1,116	1,204	1,365
CASH AVAILABLE		3,928	3,061	4,137	4,616	4,606	3,843
CASH BALANCE (BEGINNING)			1,454	1,159	1,147	1,899	2,923
TOTAL DEBT SERVICE		2,475	3,356	4,149	3,864	3,581	4,042
INTEREST :							
- LONG TERM LOAN :		1,040	972	814	629	447	264
- SHORT TERM LOAN		434	384	334	234	134	34
REPAYMENT :							
- LONG TERM LOAN :		500	1,500	2,000	2,000	2,000	3,399
- SHORT TERM LOAN		500	500	1,000	1,000	1,000	344
CASH BALANCE (ENDING)		1,454	1,159	1,147	1,899	2,923	2,724
CASH EXCESS/(DEFISIT)		1,454	(295)	(12)	752	1,024	(200)

APPENDIX-3
CHEMICAL INDUSTRIES Ltd.
PROFIT & LOSS PROJECTION

IN 000 US$

ITEMS		Year 0	Year 1	Year 2	Year 3	Year 4	Year 5	Year 6
SALES :								
SALES OF PRODUCTS			32,116	39,495	46,100	48,620	51,051	53,604
COST OF GOODS SOLD			27,803	33,831	39,254	41,417	43,554	45,851
GROSS PROFIT			4,313	5,665	6,846	7,203	7,498	7,753
GEN & ADM. EXPENSE			1,192	1,339	1,506	1,695	1,908	2,148
SELLING EXPENSES			380	429	485	548	620	701
GEN & ADM. DEPRECIATION			33	33	33	33	33	53
AMORTIZATION			344	344	344	344	344	
OPERATING INCOME			2,365	3,519	4,479	4,584	4,594	4,850
INTEREST EXPENSE :								
- LONG TERM LOAN			1,040	972	814	629	447	264
- SHORT TERM LOAN			434	384	334	234	134	34
EARNING BEFORE TAX			890	2,163	3,330	3,720	4,012	4,551
INCOME TAX	30.00%		267	649	999	1,116	1,204	1,365
NET PROFIT/LOSS			623	1,514	2,331	2,604	2,809	3,186
DIVIDEND								
RETAINED EARNINGS			623	2,137	4,468	7,072	9,880	13,066

APPENDIX-4
CHEMICAL INDUSTRIES Ltd.
COST OF GOODS SOLD

IN 000 US$

ITEMS	Year 0	Year 1	Year 2	Year 3	Year 4	Year 5	Year 6
RAW MATERIALS :							
FIRST OF THE YEAR							
PA + 2 EH			2,240	2,646	3,087	3,241	3,403
PURCHASES							
PA + 2 EH		29,120	32,046	37,353	38,896	40,841	42,883
END OF THE YEAR							
PA + 2 EH		(2,240)	(2,646)	(3,087)	(3,241)	(3,403)	(3,574)
TOTAL RAW MATERIALS USED		26,880	31,640	36,912	38,742	40,679	42,713
DIRECT LABOUR COST		156	179	206	237	272	313
FACTORY OVERHEAD COST		918	1,049	1,199	1,350	1,521	1,731
FACTORY DEPRECIATION		1,186	1,186	1,186	1,186	1,186	1,206
TOTAL PRODUCTION COST		29,140	34,054	39,502	41,514	43,657	45,963
GOODS IN PROCESS :							
FIRST OF THE YEAR			73	85	99	104	109
END OF THE YEAR		(73)	(85)	(99)	(104)	(109)	(115)
COST OF GOODS MANUFACTURED		29,067	34,042	39,488	41,509	43,652	45,957
FINISHED GOODS :							
FIRST OF THE YEAR			1,264	1,475	1,709	1,800	1,899
END OF THE YEAR		(1,264)	(1,475)	(1,709)	(1,800)	(1,899)	(2,005)
COST OF GOODS SOLD OF PRODUCTS		27,803	33,831	39,254	41,417	43,554	45,851

APPENDIX-5
CHEMICAL INDUSTRIES Ltd.
PRODUCTION, SALES AND COLLECTION SCHEDULE   IN 000 US$

ITEMS	Year 0	Year 1	Year 2	Year 3	Year 4	Year 5	Year 6
PRODUCTION (MTPA):							
Plasticizer		24,000	27,000	30,000	30,000	30,000	30,000
GOODS IN PROCESS (MTPA):							
FIRST OF THE YEAR:							
Plasticizer			60	68	75	75	75
END OF THE YEAR:							
Plasticizer		(60)	(68)	(75)	(75)	(75)	(75)
FINISHED GOODS (MTPA):							
FIRST OF THE YEAR:							
Plasticizer			1,000	1,125	1,250	1,250	1,250
END OF THE YEAR:							
Plasticizer		(1,000)	(1,125)	(1,250)	(1,250)	(1,250)	(1,250)
TOTAL SALES VOLUME (MTPA)							
Plasticizer		22,940	26,868	29,868	30,000	30,000	30,000
SALES VALUE (US$)							
Plasticizer		32,116	39,495	46,100	48,620	51,051	53,604
TOTAL SALES OF PRODUCTS (US$)		32,116	39,495	46,100	48,620	51,051	53,604
ACCOUNTS RECEIVABLE:							
FIRST OF THE YEAR			5,353	6,583	7,683	8,103	8,509
END OF THE YEAR		(5,353)	(6,583)	(7,683)	(8,103)	(8,509)	(8,934)
A/R COLLECTION		26,763	38,265	45,000	48,200	50,646	53,178

LAMPIRAN V-6

CHEMICAL INDUSTRIES Ltd.

STRUCTURE OF FUNDS, LOAN DISBURSEMENT AND REPAYMENT SCHEDULE   IN 000 US$

ITEMS	Total	Year 0	Year 1	Year 2	Year 3	Year 4	Year 5	Year 6
EQUITY	4,674	4,674						
- INVESTMENT	4,674	4,674						
- WORKING CAPITAL								
LOAN	15,743	11,399	4,344					
- LONG TERM LOAN :	11,399	11,399						
INVESTMENT	10,493	10,493						
I. D. C.	906	906						
- SHORT TERM LOAN	4,344		4,344					
REPAYMENT								
- LONG TERM LOAN :	11,399		500	1,500	2,000	2,000	2,000	3,399
- SHORT TERM LOAN	4,344		500	500	1,000	1,000	1,000	344
BALANCE								
- LONG TERM LOAN	47,894	11,399	10,899	9,399	7,399	5,399	3,399	
- SHORT TERM LOAN	11,222		3,844	3,344	2,344	1,344	344	
INTEREST	5,723		1,475	1,356	1,149	864	581	299
- LONG TERM LOAN :	4,167		1,040	972	814	629	447	264
- SHORT TERM LOAN	1,557		434	384	334	234	134	34

APPENDIX-7
CHEMICAL INDUSTRIES Ltd.
DRAW DOWN OF PROJECT COST SCHEDULE

IN 000 US$

No.	Description	Amount US$	(%)	Year - I				Year - II	
				Q-1	Q-2	Q-3	Q-4	Q-1	Q-2
A I	Land:								
1	Land Cost	2,500	15.55%	2,500					
2	Land Improvement	2,000	12.44%	1,000	1,000				
II	Construction:								
2	ISBL	5,600	34.84%			1,120	1,960	1,960	560
3	OSBL	3,924	24.41%			785	1,373	1,373	392
4	Vehicle	144	0.90%			36	36	36	36
5	Tool & Office Equip.	187	1.17%			47	47	47	47
	Total A	14,356	89.31%	3,500	1,000	1,988	3,416	3,416	1,035
B	Pre-Operating:								
	Technical Asst. & Training	150	0.93%	23	23	30	30	23	23
	Project Management Cost	250	1.56%	38	38	50	50	38	38
	Start-up & Commissioning	100	0.62%	15	15	20	20	15	15
	Others	135	0.84%	20	20	27	27	20	20
	Total B	635	3.95%	95	95	127	127	95	95
	Total Before IDC (A+B)	14,991	93.26%	3,595	1,095	2,115	3,543	3,512	1,131

Continue of APPENDIX-7

IN 000 US$

No.	Description	Amount US$	(%)	Year - I				Year - II	
				Q-1	Q-2	Q-3	Q-4	Q-1	Q-2
C	Others:								
	IDC	906	5.63%	57	77	113	172	232	255
	Management Fee	52	0.33%	52					
	Commitment Fee	125	0.78%	40	36	29	16	4	
	Total C	1,083	6.74%	149	113	141	188	236	255
	Grand Total	16,073	100.00%	3,744	1,208	2,256	3,732	3,748	1,386
D	Portion of Investment								
I	Bank Loan:								
	Investment	10,493	70.00%	2,517	767	1,480	2,480	2,458	791
	I. D. C.	906		57	77	113	172	232	255
	Total	11,399		2,573	843	1,593	2,652	2,690	1,047
II	Equity:								
	Investment	4,497	30.00%	1,079	329	634	1,063	1,053	339
	Management Fee	52	0.50%	52					
	Commitment Fee	125	0.50%	40	36	29	16	4	
	Total	4,674		1,171	365	663	1,079	1,057	339
	Total Bank + Equity	16,073		3,744	1,208	2,256	3,732	3,748	1,386

APPENDIX-7A
CHEMICAL INDUSTRIES Ltd.
INTEREST DURING CONSTRUCTION (IDC)

PERIOD	Cash Withdrawl	Total Loan 70.00%	Balance	Accumulation Loan	Interest Rate 9.00%	Accumulation Interest	Interest from Interest	I D C 8.63%
YEAR-I			10,493					
Q-1	3,595	2,517	7,977	2,517	57	57		57
Q-2	1,095	767	7,210	3,283	74	131	3	77
Q-3	2,115	1,480	5,730	4,764	107	238	5	113
Q-4	3,543	2,480	3,249	7,244	163	401	9	172
YEAR-II								
Q-1	3,512	2,458	791	9,702	218	619	14	232
Q-2	1,131	791	0	10,493	236	855	19	255
	14,991	10,493		38,003	855	2,300	50	906

APPENDIX-8
CHEMICAL INDUSTRIES Ltd.
INVESTMENT AND REINTVESMENT SCHEDULE

IN 000 US$

ITEMS	TOTAL	Year 0	Year 1	Year 2	Year 3	Year 4	Year 5	Year 6
FIXED ASSETS :								
LAND COST	2,500	2,500						
LAND IMPROVEMENT	2,000	2,000						
I. S. B. L.	5,600	5,600						
O. S. B. L.	3,924	3,924						
Vehicle	376	144						232
Tool & Office Equip.	489	187						302
TOTAL FIXED ASSETS	14,890	14,356						534
OTHERS ASSET :								
PREOPERATING EXPENSES	635	635						
I D C + MGT & COMT FEE	1,083	1,083						
TOTAL OTHER ASSETS	1,718	1,718						
TOTAL INVESTMENT	16,607	16,073						534
WORKING CAPITAL LOAN	4,344		4,344					
TOTAL PROJECT COST	20,952	16,073	4,344					534
ACCUM. PROJECT COST		16,073	20,418	20,418	20,418	20,418	20,418	20,952

APPENDIX-9
CHEMICAL INDUSTRIES Ltd.
DEPRECIATION AND MAINTENANCE SCHEDULE   IN 000 US$

ITEMS	TOTAL	Year 0	Year 1	Year 2	Year 3	Year 4	Year 5	Year 6
DEPRECIATION :								
FACTORY								
LAND IMPROVEMENT	2,000		200	200	200	200	200	200
I. S. B. L.	5,600		560	560	560	560	560	560
O. S. B. L.	3,924		392	392	392	392	392	392
Vehicle	188		14	14	14	14	14	23
Tool & Office Equip.	245		19	19	19	19	19	30
TOTAL	11,957		1,186	1,186	1,186	1,186	1,186	1,206
GEN & ADM. DEPRECIATION								
Vehicle	188		14	14	14	14	14	23
Tools & Office Equip.	245		19	19	19	19	19	30
TOTAL			33	33	33	33	33	53
TOTAL DEPRECIATION			1,219	1,219	1,219	1,219	1,219	1,259

Continue of APPENDIX-9

IN 000 US$

ITEMS	TOTAL	Year 0	Year 1	Year 2	Year 3	Year 4	Year 5	Year 6
AMORTIZATION :								
PREOPERATING COST	635		127	127	127	127	127	
I D C MGT & COMT FEE	1,083		217	217	217	217	217	
TOTAL	1,718		344	344	344	344	344	
TOTAL DEPR. + AMORT.	13,675		1,529	1,529	1,529	1,529	1,529	1,206
MAINTENANCE COST								
FACTORY:								
LAND IMPROVEMENT	1.00%		16	20	24	27	29	32
I. S. B. L.	1.00%		45	55	68	75	82	90
O. S. B. L.	1.50%		47	58	71	78	86	95
Vehicle	2.00%		2	3	3	4	4	12
Tool & Office Equip.	2.00%		3	4	5	5	5	16
TOTAL			113	140	171	188	207	245

APPENDIX-10
CHEMICAL INDUSTRIES Ltd.
CASH REQUIREMENT FOR OPERATION

IN 000 US$

ITEMS	Year 0	Year 1	Year 2	Year 3	Year 4	Year 5	Year 6
DIRECT LABOUR COST		156	179	206	237	272	313
FACTORY OVERHEAD COST							
IND. LABOUR		472	543	624	718	826	949
MAINTENANCE		113	140	171	188	207	245
INSURANCE		51	56	62	68	75	82
CONSUMMABLE		36	40	43	48	53	58
WATER		23	26	28	31	34	38
CHEMICAL		24	26	29	32	35	39
TRANSPORTATION		24	26	29	32	35	39
LEASE FOR LAND		100	110	121	133	146	161
PHONE, WATER & LIGHT		50	55	61	67	73	81
MISCELLANEOUS		25	28	30	33	37	40
TOTAL		918	1,049	1,199	1,350	1,521	1,731

Continue of APPENDIX-10

IN 000 US$

ITEMS	Year 0	Year 1	Year 2	Year 3	Year 4	Year 5	Year 6
GENERAL & ADM. EXP.							
WAGES & SALARIES		572	658	756	870	1,000	1,150
PROSPERITY FUND		87	96	105	116	128	140
OFFICE RENTAL		400	440	484	532	586	644
PHONE, WATER & LIGHT		36	40	43	48	53	58
TRANSPORTATION		53	59	64	71	78	86
OFFICE EXPENSES		33	37	40	44	49	54
OTHERS		10	11	12	13	15	16
TOTAL		1,192	1,339	1,506	1,695	1,908	2,148
TOTAL OPERATION COST		1,074	1,228	1,404	1,586	1,793	2,044
ESTIMATED CASH REQUIREMENT		269	307	351	397	448	511
SELLING EXPENSES							
WAGES		222	255	293	337	388	446
OFFICE STATIONERIES		13	15	16	18	19	21
PHONE, WATER & LIGHT		67	73	80	89	97	107
LABOUR INSURANCE		3	4	4	4	5	5
OFFICE RENTAL		48	53	58	64	70	77
MEDICAL ALLOWANCES		6	6	7	7	8	9
OTHERS		22	24	27	29	32	35
TOTAL		380	429	485	548	620	701

APPENDIX-11
CHEMICAL INDUSTRIES Ltd.
ESTIMATED WORKING CAPITAL NEEDED   IN 000 US$

ITEMS	Year 0	Year 1	Year 2	Year 3	Year 4	Year 5	Year 6
ACCOUNTS RECEIVABLE		5,353	6,583	7,683	8,103	8,509	8,934
INVENTORIES :							
RAW MATERIALS		2,240	2,646	3,087	3,241	3,403	3,574
GOODS IN PROCESS		73	85	99	104	109	115
FINISHED GOODS		1,264	1,475	1,709	1,800	1,899	2,005
CASH REQUIREMENT		269	307	351	397	448	511
TOTAL REQUIREMENT		9,198	11,095	12,929	13,645	14,368	15,138
ACCOUNTS PAYABLE							
- IMPORT							
- LOCAL		(4,853)	(5,341)	(6,225)	(6,483)	(6,807)	(7,147)
TOTAL ACCOUNTS PAYABLE		(4,853)	(5,341)	(6,225)	(6,483)	(6,807)	(7,147)
NET WORKING CAPITAL		4,344	5,754	6,703	7,163	7,561	7,991
INCREASE (DECREASE) OF ACCOUNTS PAY.		4,853	488	884	257	324	340
INCREASE (DECREASE) OF WORK. CAPITAL		4,344	1,410	949	459	398	430

APPENDIX-12
CHEMICAL INDUSTRIES Ltd.
FINANCIAL RATIO

IN 000 US$

ITEMS	Year 0	Year 1	Year 2	Year 3	Year 4	Year 5	Year 6
PAYBACK PERIOD :							
INVESTMENT	(16,073)	(16,073)	(16,073)	(16,073)	(16,073)	(16,073)	(16,607)
DIVIDEN							
RETAINED EARNING		623	2,137	4,468	7,072	9,880	13,066
INTEREST EXPENSES		1,475	2,831	3,979	4,843	5,425	5,723
DEPRECIATION & AMORTIZATION		1,562	3,125	4,687	6,249	7,811	9,071
INVESTMENT - (PROFIT+AMORT.+DEPR.)	(16,073)	(12,414)	(7,981)	(2,939)	2,091	7,043	11,253
CURRENT RATIO : - CURRENT ASSETS		10,383	11,947	13,725	15,148	16,843	17,351
- CURRENT LIABILITIES		8,698	8,685	8,570	7,827	7,151	7,147
(CURRENT ASSETS:CURRENT LIAB.) * 100%		119.38%	137.55%	160.15%	193.53%	235.52%	242.77%
PROFIT MARGIN - NET PROFIT		623	1,514	2,331	2,604	2,809	3,186
- SALES		32,116	39,495	46,100	48,620	51,051	53,604
(NET PROFIT : SALES) X 100%		1.94%	3.83%	5.06%	5.36%	5.50%	5.94%
R. O. I. : - OPERATING INCOME		2,365	3,519	4,479	4,584	4,594	4,850
- TOTAL ASSETS		24,894	24,896	25,111	24,972	25,105	24,888
(OPERAT. INCOME:TOTAL ASSETS) X 100%		9.50%	14.14%	17.83%	18.36%	18.30%	19.49%

Continue of APPENDIX-12

ITEMS		Year 0	Year 1	Year 2	Year 3	Year 4	Year 5	Year 6
R. O. E. : - NET INCOME			623	1,514	2,331	2,604	2,809	3,186
- EQUITY			5,297	6,812	9,142	11,746	14,555	17,741
(NET INCOME : EQUITY) X100%			11.76%	22.23%	25.50%	22.17%	19.30%	17.96%
DEBT TO EQUITY RATIO :- LIABILITIES		11,399	19,597	18,084	15,969	13,226	10,550	7,147
- EQUITY		4,674	5,297	6,812	9,142	11,746	14,555	17,741
(LIABILITIES : EQUITY) X 100%		243.86%	369.93%	265.50%	174.67%	112.60%	72.49%	40.29%
DEBT TO TOTAL ASSETS :- LIABILITIES		11,399	19,597	18,084	15,969	13,226	10,550	7,147
- TOTAL ASSETS		16,073	24,894	24,896	25,111	24,972	25,105	24,888
(LIABILITIES : TOTAL ASSETS) X 100%		70.92%	78.72%	72.64%	63.59%	52.96%	42.02%	28.72%
BREAK EVEN POINT :								
TOTAL REVENUE	A		32,116	39,495	46,100	48,620	51,051	53,604
TOTAL VARIABLE COST	B		27,351	33,382	38,884	41,137	43,384	45,777
CONTRIBUTION MARGIN	C		4,765	6,113	7,216	7,483	7,667	7,827
FIXED COST	D		3,762	4,170	4,400	4,331	4,239	3,940
PRODUCTION PLANNING E (MTPA)			24,000	27,000	30,000	30,000	30,000	30,000
BREAK EVEN POINT (%)	D/(A-B)		78.946%	68.208%	60.978%	57.875%	55.284%	50.338%
BREAK EVEN POINT (MT)	(D/(A-B))*E		18,947	18,416	18,293	17,362	16,585	15,101
BREAK EVEN POINT (US$)	D/(1-(B/A))		25,354	26,939	28,111	28,139	28,223	26,983

APPENDIX-13
CHEMICAL INDUSTRIES Ltd.
INTERNAL RATE OF RETURN

IN 000 US$

ITEMS	Year 0	Year 1	Year 2	Year 3	Year 4	Year 5	Year 6
IRR ON EBIT (NET PROFIT)							
INVESTMENT (EQUITY + L/T LOAN)	(16,073)						
WORKING CAP. (EQUITY + S/T LOAN)		(4,344)					
NET PROFIT		623	1,514	2,331	2,604	2,809	3,186
DEPRECIATION & AMORTIZATION		1,529	1,529	1,529	1,529	1,529	1,206
INTEREST EXPENSE		1,475	1,356	1,149	864	581	299
INCOME TAX		267	649	999	1,116	1,204	1,365
SALVAGE VALUE							
IRR = 24.68%	(16,073)	(451)	5,048	6,008	6,113	6,123	6,056

APPENDIX-14
CHEMICAL INDUSTRIES Ltd.
SENSITIVITY ANALYSIS

Sales Price	IRR	Raw Material Cost	IRR	Production Cost	IRR	Production Quanity (MTPA)	IRR	Investment Cost	IRR
-5.00%	6.29%	-5.00%	34.43%	-5.00%	26.85%	50.00%	-37.62%	-5.00%	26.10%
-4.00%	10.00%	-4.00%	32.56%	-4.00%	26.43%	55.00%	-15.09%	-4.00%	25.81%
-3.00%	14.11%	-3.00%	30.66%	-3.00%	26.00%	60.00%	-6.84%	-3.00%	25.52%
-2.00%	17.78%	-2.00%	28.71%	-2.00%	25.57%	65.00%	-1.20%	-2.00%	25.24%
-1.00%	20.67%	-1.00%	26.72%	-1.00%	25.13%	70.00%	3.27%	-1.00%	24.96%
	24.68%		24.68%		24.68%	75.00%	7.30%		24.68%
1.00%	27.19%	1.00%	21.16%	1.00%	24.22%	80.00%	10.81%	1.00%	24.41%
2.00%	29.62%	2.00%	18.82%	2.00%	22.33%	85.00%	14.86%	2.00%	24.14%
3.00%	31.97%	3.00%	16.23%	3.00%	21.86%	90.00%	18.11%	3.00%	23.87%
4.00%	34.27%	4.00%	12.70%	4.00%	21.37%	95.00%	20.84%	4.00%	23.61%
5.00%	36.51%	5.00%	9.80%	5.00%	20.88%	100.00%	24.68%	5.00%	23.35%

THE AUTHOR

Ir. Harmaizar Zaharuddin, is born at August 25 1964 in Curup of Bengkulu province, Indonesia, is a specialist in Investment Management and Feasibility Study and is a member MAPPI (Appraisal Profession Society of Indonesia) as well. He has got his scholar at Indonesia University, the faculty of technique in major of Industrial Engineering in 1991. Besides that, he has participated in various trainings and seminars that were related to the investment and financial management.

Experiences:

In1989 (the practical job). He succeeded applying the theory of Queue and Balance of Production Track by increasing the rather significant production volume at Panca Motor Ltd. (Isuzu Truck Assembling).

1990-1992, joined in Appraisal Consultant on Feasibility Study Division.

1992-1999, joined at Eternal Buana Chemical Industries (EBCI) Ltd., in Business Development division, headed Feasibility Study and Budget Control section. Early in the joining, there was only one company. Then, together with one team, we succeeded expanding the company which 15 companies have been operating, 5 companies are still developing and ±10 companies are still in analysis process. And we also brought one of Holding Companies to Go Public / Initial Public Overing (IPO), namely, Eterindo Wahanatama Plc. (ETWA). All the companies (that realized ones, in planning and IPO) are located in some countries, such as: Indonesia, Singapore, Malaysia, Thailand, Hongkong and China. The investments are funded by some investors and investors' representative, namely:

- Local Investors: BNI46, BII, HSBC, Bank Bali, Standard Chartered Bank, BHS, ABN-AMRO Bank, Deutsche Bank, Prima Express Bank, Petrokimia Ltd., Tirtamas Majutama Ltd. (Polytama Propindo Ltd.), Witulan Ltd., Justus Kimia Raya Ltd.,

Schroders, Bank Niaga, Mitsubishi Buana Bank, Sejahtera Bank Umum, Fuji Bank International, Vickers Ballas, etc

- Foreign Investments: Mitsui & Co. Ltd., HSBC (Hongkong), Mitsui Bussan Solvent & Coating Co. Ltd., Kyowa Hakko Kogyo Co. Ltd., Daewo, Union Bank of Switzerland (UBS-Singapore), Suez Asia Holding PTE. Ltd, Bankers Trust Company, Search Investment Office PTE Ltd, Stevenloh, Singapore Institute of Surveyors and Valuer, AMMB International, etc.

1999 – Up to now:

- Being active in Investment Management and Project of the Feasibility Study, giving some companies for trainings and teaching at some universities as well.

- The writer has ever made more than 100 projects of the Feasibility Study; they are the new investments, expanding, acquisition, Analysis of Working Capital Need, or Go-Public / Initial Public Overing (IPO).

- Being active in Public Organization (ORMAS); Nation Volunteer (RB) as the chairman of Facilitation of Micro, Small and Medium Entrepreneurs (UMKM) Department.

BOOKS OF HARMAIZAR

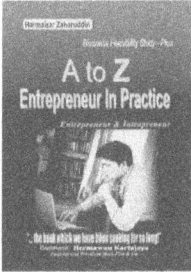

A to Z Entrepreneur in Practice: Business Feasibility Study

The New Concept **IACM** (Investment Analysis Chain Metohd) facilitate operate your business or school

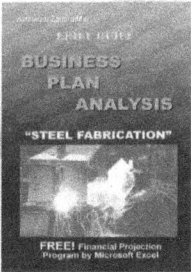

Busines Plan Analysis for **"Steel Fabrication"**: Busines Credit Plan & Proposal

FREE!, Financial Projection Program by Microsoft Excel

Busines Plan Analysis for **"Chemical Industries"**: Busines Credit Plan & Proposal

FREE!, Financial Projection Program by Microsoft Excel

BUSINESS PLAN ANALYSIS for **"Mini Market / Shop"**: Busines Credit Plan & Proposal

FREE!, Financial Projection Program by Microsoft Excel

BOOKS OF HARMAIZAR

BUSINESS PLAN ANALYSIS for "**Export - Import**": Busines Credit Plan & Proposal

FREE!, Financial Projection Program by Microsoft Excel

BUSINESS PLAN ANALYSIS for "**Agent &Distributor**": Busines Credit Plan & Proposal

FREE!, Financial Projection Program by Microsoft Excel

BUSINESS PLAN ANALYSIS for "**HP Kiosk & Refill Mineral Water**": Busines Credit Plan & Proposal

FREE!, Financial Projection Program by Microsoft Excel

Application of "BID DOCUMENTS": within Invitation To Bid (ITB), For **Prosess Design Package (PDP) & Engineering Procurement Contract (EPC).**

Specialist for Technologies: Treat and Fabrication Industries.

9789799799449